EVERYMAN A BIBLE STUDENT

"Have you got a reasonably-sized book written in simple terms that will help me to understand the Bible?" This is one of the most frequently-asked questions in a Christian bookshop, and you are holding the answer in your hands. For Dr. Joe Church's *Everyman a Bible Student* has, over the past 26 years, answered this question for over 70,000 readers—and the demand still continues. But times and language change. So *Everyman a Bible Student* has been completely re-cast, revised and very considerably enlarged, so that many more thousands of readers may find it to be the channel which leads them into a deeper understanding of God's word written, and to a commitment to its precepts.

By the same author:

AWAKE! UGANDA
JESUS SATISFIES
FORGIVE THEM: An African Martyr (*with others*)
OUT OF THE PIT

Everyman a Bible Student

A Handbook of Basic Bible Doctrines

by

J. E. Church

ZONDERVAN
PUBLISHING HOUSE

OF THE ZONDERVAN CORPORATION | GRAND RAPIDS, MICHIGAN 49506

Copyright © *The Paternoster Press Ltd.*, *1976*
Original edition, 1938. Reprinted 17 times between 1938 and
1976. ISBN: 85364 189 7

First Zondervan printing 1977

Reprinted by special arrangement with
The Paternoster Press

Library of Congress Cataloging in Publication Data

Church, John Edward.
Everyman a Bible student.

1. Bible — Indexes, Topical.   I. Title.
BS432.C553   1977   220.2   77-4326

ISBN 0-310-35651-2

Printed in the United States of America

I DEDICATE THIS BOOK
TO MY WIFE
DECIE
AND TO THE
AFRICANS
ESPECIALLY
SIMEONI NSIBAMBI
BLASIO KIGOZI
YOSIYA KINUKA
WILLIAM NAGENDA
AND
ERIKA SABITI
WHO, OVER THE YEARS, HELPED
ME TO MAKE THESE SUBJECTS
REAL
IN EVERY DAY LIVING

CONTENTS

Publishers' Foreword 9

Preface 11

The Bible Today 13

How to use this book 15

Abbreviations 17

1 GOD: The Supreme Being 19

2 MAN: The Human Race 21

3 SIN: Evil 23

4 CHRIST: The Lord Jesus 25

5 REPENTANCE: Change of heart 28

6 REPENTANCE: Confession of sin 30

7 FAITH: Trust in Jesus 32

8 ATONEMENT: at-one-ment 34

9 SACRIFICE: Dying for the human race 36

10 REDEMPTION: Buying back 38

11 JUSTIFICATION: Acquittal 39

12 THE GOSPEL: Good News 40

13 FORGIVENESS: Set free 42

14 ETERNAL LIFE: Lasting for ever 44

15 THE KINGDOM OF HEAVEN: The Kingdom of God 46

16 ASSURANCE: Confidence 48

17 TEMPTATION AND TESTING 50

18 SATAN: The Evil One 52

19 SALVATION: The Cross 54

20 SALVATION: The New Birth 57

21 PRAYER: Communication with God 59

22 COMPROMISE: Separation from the world 61

23 THE WILDERNESS LIFE: The "Up and Down" Life 63

24 THE VICTORIOUS LIFE: "Not I but Christ" 65

25 THE HOLY SPIRIT: The Third Person of the Trinity 69

26 THE HOLY SPIRIT: The Fullness 72

CONTENTS (*Continued*)

27 SANCTIFICATION: The Highway of Holiness   75
28 LOVE: The Love of God   77
29 LIGHT: Life in the Light   79
30 FELLOWSHIP: Oneness   81
31 LAW: Works   84
32 GRACE: The unmerited love of God   85
33 APOSTASY: "falling away"   88
34 THE PROBLEM OF PAIN AND SUFFERING   91
35 HEALING: Physical and Spiritual   93
36 DEATH: Physical and Spiritual   95
37 THE PROBLEM OF ADDICTION: alcohol, drugs, gambling   97
38 PRIESTHOOD: and Ministry   100
39 RESURRECTION: Coming back to life   103
40 THE AFTER-LIFE: Hell   105
41 THE AFTER-LIFE: Heaven   106
42 BAPTISM: Initiation   108
43 THE LORD'S SUPPER: Holy Communion   111
44 THE BIBLE: Inspiration   114
45 THE CHURCH: Invisible and Visible   117
46 CALL TO MISSION: "Here am I, send me"   120
47 THE SECOND ADVENT: The Second Coming of Christ   122

PUBLISHERS' FOREWORD TO THE SECOND EDITION

Among the more significant trends in the world of books today is the apparently inexhaustible demand for modern versions of the Bible. In many universities the Christian Union is the best-supported student society and one of its most basic activities is Bible study. The Roman Catholic Church which for centuries did not encourage lay members to read the Bible by themselves now welcomes the existence of thousands of Bible study groups and has itself produced an outstanding modern version. Even behind the Iron Curtain public interest in the Bible is recognised by the very fact that quantities are severely limited since the authorities are apparently unwilling to let it circulate freely. Some Christians in China are reduced to taking it down in longhand as it is read from Christian broadcasting stations.

What are all these readers seeking? To answer with a negative: what they are *not* seeking is a series of sermons from a preacher "six feet above contradiction". Nor are they in the market for a mass of inert academic information about the Bible. What they want is to find out for themselves the message of the Bible, to discover the secret of its extraordinary power to change lives and restore relationships, to lift the burden of guilt, to bring peace and joy to sad and restless people. In fact, although they may not consciously realise this, they want to hear God speaking personally to them. In spite of the fact that this is rarely a wholly comfortable experience, they are prepared to go through with it because they know, with growing certainty, that in studying the Bible they are in touch with Reality.

The reasons for this interest are not very difficult to distinguish. One is a concern that underlies and reinforces the "Doomwatch" fears of Western man. When everything possible has been said about the problems of pollution, dwindling supplies of fuel and raw materials, the population explosion, the losing fight against famine—there still remains another problem equally grave. For the trouble does not derive only from man's environment; he himself is malfunctioning as seriously as any rogue space-craft. Behind all the prophecies of the futurologists looms the threatening suspicion that man will never set his environment to rights until his own defects have been made good.

Despite the efforts of an army of psychiatrists, the number of patients receiving treatment for mental and emotional illness soars. Frequently the root of the problem is something as ancient as the Book of Genesis, the theme of novels and plays since literature began—guilt, often repressed but still active.

Family life, which has traditionally been regarded as a source of strength and support, is nowadays too often a focus of stress and unhappiness. Broken homes are only the tip of an iceberg of misery and frustration which has led some vocal individuals to clamour for the abolition of the family. A century ago it might have seemed that the prospect of cheap food, technological advance and universal education would exorcise fear of the future from the mind of Western man. But today many people are desperately afraid of the future, not merely because of the horrifying possibilities of modern warfare but also because of the very real danger of famine and the constant threat of revolution whether from Right or Left— whatever this distinction may mean.

In addition a new and profoundly disturbing type of stress is being experienced wherever social change is demolishing established structures. As former skills once valued (and as various as blacksmithing and shorthand) become unnecessary, as relationships become less easy to define—and who today can prescribe the role of a father, a teacher, a minister?—so westernised man faces what is often called an identity crisis. To some readers of these pages it will seem all but incredible that any sane human being could ever seriously ask the question "Who am I?"; but many others will recognise it as one that has perplexed them for as long as they can remember.

It confronted Dietrich Bonhoeffer for example, when he was imprisoned by the Nazis for opposing Hitler. As he faced death, Bonhoeffer, bewildered by the inner contradiction of his personality, asked

> "Who am I? They mock me,
> these lonely questions of mine.
> Whoever I am, thou
> knowest, O God, I am thine."

It is significant that Bonhoeffer found the answer to his search in his relationship with God. For today there is a world-wide revival of interest in religion. Not necessarily in religious institutions as such; many people have had more than enough of these. But in their search for an answer to life's ultimate questions, in the quest for some security in an unsure world, young people especially are examining the world's religions to see whether there may not be hidden in this area of human experience some way of making sense of the nonsense that men used to call the cosmos.

A correspondent from Japan tells how "this desire to know drives 16, 14 and even 12-year-olds to seriously read the works of philosophers such as Kant, Confucius and Nietzsche . . . Next to these philosophical works is the Bible."

In the light of all this, we can see why interest in the Bible is everywhere increasing. The multitude of new translations is a symptom rather than a cause. It is also obvious why Joe Church's little book has gone on being read for so many years. Why it appeals equally to Christians and would-be Christians in East Africa and in Western universities. Why people have continued using it throughout years when many far more impressive books about the Bible have appeared briefly and vanished without trace. Quite simply it aims to help people read the Bible for themselves so that they can hear God speaking to them individually. It presents basic biblical truth with a multitude of references so that readers today can emulate those of the first century AD and "study the scriptures every day to see whether" they agree with what is said about them (Acts 17:11). Mature Christians find its summary treatment of biblical themes an aid in teaching others. Young Christians and would-be Christians use it as a way of getting to grips with the biblical message.

Many hours have been spent in revising this new edition and in trying to ensure that although in some ways up-dated it should retain the qualities of simplicity, directness and transparency to the biblical theme of Salvation which have rendered it so powerful in the past. It has become a cliché to talk about the power of the printed word. But if books may have a powerful influence on human life and even on world history, how much more powerful may we hope that a book may prove to be which points the reader beyond its own pages to the Book in which God himself has spoken to the human race? If EVERY MAN A BIBLE STUDENT can go on fulfilling this John the Baptist role, then author and publishers can together exclaim *Soli Deo Gloria*.

AUTHOR'S PREFACE

This book is rooted in revival. It took shape over a number of years as an outcome of the Revival which from 1932 spread through Central and East Africa. As a result, it was found necessary to provide simplified and deeper teaching from the Word of God on the great fundamental truths of the Faith. It was in a time of renewal, and of new opportunity, a 'tide taken in the flood'.

In the preface to this new book we look back at some of the unmistakable marks of God's guiding hand since the beginning.

First was the friend of mine, when I was a medical student at Cambridge University, who led me into the thrills of Bible study following a subject or doctrine right through the Bible (actually using the Scofield Reference Bible) and then looking back to see the whole panoramic view.

Then there were the speakers, too many to number, who came up week by week to the Christian Union (the C.I.C.C.U.) and who pointed us to the Life of Victory, showing us the 'up-and-down' life in 'the wilderness' and the 'giants' that stop us entering into 'the Promised Land', and lighting up the agelong quest for holiness.

Then there was the place of prayer. On sailing for Africa as a young doctor I had the privilege of becoming the 'own missionary' of the C.I.C.C.U. and the prayer support of their daily prayer meeting. Could we ever know how much those prayers and the caring of the generations of students during the following thirty-seven years meant in the outpouring of the Holy Spirit in Ruanda and Uganda!

Here I made two important discoveries. The first of these was the power of the Holy Spirit to use the written Word alone. As an overworked missionary doctor, trying to cope with an impossible number of tasks, and not being good at the language, I found that through the simple reading of carefully chosen verses from the Bible conviction often came with repentance and sometimes with tears, faces relaxed and men found peace.

The second discovery was the strength of fellowship in team work with Africans and the breaking of the barrier between black and white. My head hospital assistant, Josiah, a life-long friend, was converted and joined me in my preaching. What I said, or tried to say, in the vernacular, he would repeat correctly, with his enthusiasm and joy, and the Holy Spirit would melt people's hearts. Interpretation enhanced the message. We would sometimes write the texts on a blackboard and perhaps draw a picture. The message went home by 'eye-gate'. The subjects of this book were taught in this way.

The hand of God was again seen in the printing of the book. As medical officer to a Swiss winter sports camp on my second furlough, sitting in the sun watching the skating, I was given a letter that had been brought out from the hotel. It was from a naval officer on a cruiser far away off the Falkland Islands in South America and re-directed to me. I opened it and there was a cheque for one hundred pounds, 'for God's work in Revival'. Beside me were sitting J. H. Hubbard and C. H. M. Foster, the secretaries of the Scripture Union, who wanted to help me with the printing of the Bible Studies. The cheque was the exact sum we had been praying for, so it changed hands. They got on with the printing and I sailed for Africa again, leaving my mother to correct the proofs in our Cambridge vicarage home.

This is an unusual book in that, following its first printing, sales, instead of running up quickly to a peak at first and then levelling off and coming to an end, did just the opposite. Demand rose steadily over the years to reach seventeen reprints and a selling rate of about five thousand copies a year. Then, rightly I think, it was decided in 1964 to make a large final seventeenth reprint of fifteen thousand copies with the prospect of updating the book and making some additions from what we had been learning over the years. By 1971 this final edition was nearly sold out, and it became clear that an attempt should be made to produce a completely revised, enlarged and updated version, to meet the increasing need.

Such are the influences leading to the writing of this book, which has been a team effort from the beginning. It is impossible to remember all the names of those over the years who have helped in advice and counsel. But of those who are theologians who have helped me as a medical doctor I must especially thank Archdeacon Harold Guillebaud, Bishop Lawrence Barham, Bishop Stephen Neill, Canon Bill Butler, Roy Hession, and many African friends, notably Archbishop Eric Sabiti. To these I must add Dr Stanley Smith, the late Dr Kenneth Moynagh and Dr Douglas Johnson for their encouragement, and more recently Mr Quintin Carr of Scripture Union.

I must mention now those who have worked on the translations of *Everyman a Bible Student* into many foreign languages. Hours have been spent by dedicated men and women over Bibles, concordances and dictionaries, in answer to God's call to send out the written word to the ends of the world. I want to thank God for fourteen completed translations, of which we have copies in our files, and for the work being undertaken on many others.

In 1972 God guided my wife and me to our retirement home at Little Shelford, in the green belt of my beloved Cambridge, and to the inspiring work of preparing this new book, again very much a team effort. I thank God for my wife's gift of meticulous care in the reading and checking and typing which have been involved, and for much of the typing which was undertaken by Mrs Sylvia Milner a member of our congregation.

It has been a real pleasure to work with The Paternoster Press, Howard and Jeremy Mudditt and Peter Cousins and their helpers, who have not spared themselves in doing much more than most publishers could be expected to do.

John Wesley, at the time when the French Revolution was threatening England and morals were at a low ebb, set about earnestly teaching the doctrinal truths of the Faith to his "classes" all over the country. Many historians say that the revival that resulted saved England. Our prayer today is that history may repeat itself in our present time of need. May God use this book of simple doctrine in some similar way as people are encouraged to come back to His Word.

18 *Church Street,*   JOE CHURCH
Little Shelford,
Cambridge, England.

THE BIBLE TODAY

The Old Testament was first written in *Hebrew*, the ancient language of the Jews, and it is well known that the greatest care was taken in the preservation of the parchments and scrolls, and in the copying of the text with the utmost accuracy by the Jewish scribes.

The oldest known translation from the original Hebrew Old Testament into *Greek* was made about 250 B.C. at Alexandria in Egypt, the centre of learning of the Jews after their temple in Jerusalem had been destroyed in 587 B.C. This translation was called the Septuagint (LXX) from the Latin 'septuaginta' meaning 'seventy', from the traditional number of the translators. By about A.D. 100 the Greek-speaking Christians had taken over the LXX within their Bible and it became a Christian book.

The New Testament came down to us in the 'common Greek', *koinē*, which was the 'lingua franca' of the Mediterranean lands in Roman times.

The recently discovered Dead Sea scrolls, some of which go back to the third century B.C., bear witness to the accuracy of the text. About six hundred years after the production of the LXX the whole Bible was translated into *Latin*, and was completed by Jerome in A.D. 405 in Italy. This came to be known as the Vulgate version, from the Latin 'vulgare'—'to make public', and it was the Bible used by the first Christians in Britain.

The dark ages

Unfortunately this Latin version could be read only by the clergy and in the monasteries, and there descended upon Europe what has been called 'the dark ages' which lasted until the end of the 8th century, when the Bible remained a hidden book to the vast majority of the people.

But a new day began gradually to dawn and there came a growing demand from the people to have the Bible in their own language. Various attempts at versions in English were made, but eventually about 1380 John Wycliffe, an Oxford theologian, set about translating the whole Bible 'into the language of the people'. He was attacked and condemned for "introducing among the multitude a book reserved exclusively for the use of the priests", and as his attackers said, "in this way the Gospel pearl was cast abroad and trodden underfoot by swine."

Such was the bigotry and misguided fanaticism of those days that some were martyred for the sake of this book. Outstanding among them was William Tyndale of Cambridge, who completed, with Coverdale and others, the translation of the New Testament into *English* about A.D. 1525, and went on to translate much of the Old Testament before he was burned at the stake as a heretic in the year A.D. 1536. His dying prayer . . . "Lord, open the King of England's eyes" . . . was answered by the coming of the Reformation. Indeed, even earlier, in 1535 Coverdale's version had begun to circulate freely by royal consent, and in the year A.D. 1538 Thomas Cromwell directed Archbishop Cranmer and the Bishops to have the Bible placed in every church of the land, and to be chained to the reading desk.

The Renaissance had burst upon Europe in the 15th century, and prepared the way for the resurgence of interest in translating the Bible. Since then the world has never been without the Bible.

Reformation in Europe comes with the open Bible

John Wycliffe, William Tyndale and Miles Coverdale are some of the immortal names who will always be remembered in connection with the printing of the early English Bibles. The Great Bible appeared first in 1538, (the large one placed in the churches), the Geneva Bible followed in 1560 and the Bishops' Bible in 1568; and then the famous King James Version (KJV) finally replaced them all in 1611. Under royal command, a team of forty-seven scholars worked for two and a half years on their revision. After 350 years it is still the most popular version throughout the world today.

Scholars of this century, following the discovery of thousands of Greek papyri, have realised more and more that the Bible was originally written in colloquial Hebrew and Greek and have set about making a number of new translations and paraphrases. The first was the *Revised Version* (RV) published in 1881 (NT) and 1885 (OT). In America the *American Standard Version* (ASV) comprising the RV with alterations preferred by the American Revision Committee, was published in 1901. This led to the *Revised Standard Version* (RSV) being brought out in 1952, which is the version used in this study book.

Many other modern translations and paraphrases have appeared in the twentieth century: 1902, Richard F. Weymouth: *The New Testament in Modern Speech*; 1926, James Moffat: *The Bible, a New Translation*; 1958, J. B. Phillips: *The New Testament in Modern English*; 1956, *The Amplified Bible*; 1966, *The Jerusalem Bible* (JB). Mention must also be made of the latest published recently: in 1970, the popular *New English Bible* (NEB) and *Good News for Modern Man, the New Testament in Today's English Version* (TEV), and in 1971, *The Living Bible Paraphrased*. Most recently in 1973, *The New International Version* (NIV) was prepared for the New Testament, and the Old Testament may be ready by 1976. All these seem to be the forerunners of the wind of revival that is blowing through the world at the present time—a time of great world need. Revival and the renewed love of the Bible always go together.

The last two hundred years have witnessed the great missionary movement and the preaching of the Gospel throughout the world, and the great revivals of Wesley, Finney, Moody and others in America and Britain, all associated with renewed love of the Bible. Hundreds of thousands of Bibles come off the press each year and with the aid of radio and television the Gospel has truly reached to the ends of the earth.

A new world darkness—people "under pressure"

A new malaise has come upon the world, especially in all the great cities. People are "under pressure"; there is no time to think about religion or the things of God.\A personal time of quiet prayer first thing in the morning is no longer a priority, Bible study is left out, and the Book of books is being neglected.

Christians cannot be deaf to the clamour of voices that pours out of the radio, T.V., and the press. Continually they hear scientists arguing that the existence of God cannot be proved; Marxists denying Him altogether; neo-rationalists claiming that man's reason and not the Bible is the safest guide to life, and pessimists and nihilists who affirm that God is dead.

So young and old alike are turning to mirages, to astrology, spiritism, transcendental meditation, drug experience and sex-worship. The result is that the Book that is vital to our very lives is laid aside and discredited, and in some parts of the world violently attacked. Men are forgetting that within the pages of the Bible there is to be found the secret of rest of soul, for every man and woman. They have lost sight of the Holy Spirit's power to reveal its meaning, in every age, to the humblest reader who finds time to come to God with an open mind and a hungry heart.

HOW TO USE THIS BOOK

The subjects

These are given in consecutive order beginning with God, then Man, and then Sin. A problem arose about the right order for the subjects; should Prayer precede Faith, should Grace come before or after The Cross? There is no "right order", as each subject is intimately bound up with the others. The facets of a cut and polished jewel provide a better simile, with the Holy Spirit lighting up each facet as we come to it, the jewel being Christ Himself. This fact should be borne in mind all the time a subject is being studied or expounded.

The presentation and lay-out of the subject

The subject-title heads the page and below it in simplified language is a short description of its meaning. Then come references from the O.T. in Biblical order, as far as possible, and then follows the N.T., leading up to the *Christology*—how Christ is fulfilled in it, and lastly the personal application, how it relates today to the reader.

We have tried to arrange the subjects on the pages so that when the book is open for teaching or group study, the whole subject, or a major portion of it, can be seen at a glance.

The panoramic view of the subject

No subject in the Bible can be understood intelligently apart from its position in the whole. The references are chosen therefore, wherever possible from Genesis to Revelation, the whole subject then being seen in panoramic view and thus over-emphasis on single texts avoided. "And beginning with Moses and àll the prophets, he interpreted to them in all the scriptures the things concerning himself" (Luke 24:27).

It is very important *always* to read the preceding and following verses of each reference being studied. It has been said, "A text without a context can be a pretext."

Exegesis made easy

Exegesis comes from the Greek word "*ex-hegomai*" to "lead out of" or "to expound"; that is the object of this book, to help busy everyday people into the joys of Bible study.

To make exegesis easier we have introduced the "clues" after each Bible reference, to remind the reader of the verse in question.

We aim at the minimum of comment or explanation, so that the texts, taken in order, may speak for themselves.

For personal prayer time, daily Bible study, and Scripture teaching for groups.

The subjects can be followed through, taking a few verses each day, in the individual's prayer time and Bible study, or in Bible classes. In this way a subject can be studied methodically, with growing interest, right through the Bible. These prepared studies will be found valuable for busy ministers, preachers and teachers, and also for students in centres of higher education. The world is hungry for simplified Bible teaching and is tired of mere technicalities or rhetoric.

The use of the blackboard, overhead projector, and visual aids

It has been found useful to use a blackboard when teaching from these Bible studies, writing a summary as you go along. Also simple "pin-men" drawings can make the subject live, such as a man at the bottom of a deep pit to illustrate the Fall, with a Cross at the top and a scarlet rope attached to the Cross and reaching right down to the bottom of the pit to where the man is. More recently the overhead projector has been used, drawing as the lesson proceeds, with the picture reflected on a screen behind.

Group Bible Study and House Meetings

These Bible Studies have grown up out of conventions, fellowship meetings, and house groups over the years, and have been discussed and prayed over by many. They have also travelled to many parts of the world in the eighteen reprints of the first edition of this book, so we are encouraged to stress their use for Group Bible Study especially as the winds of revival are blowing through the world again and people are turning to their Bibles for help.

We believe this is the way of the early Church, which "continued stead-fastly in the apostles' doctrine and fellowship" (Acts 2:42, KJV).

The Bible is a means of grace, and if we come to it with believing hearts and hungry souls we shall receive the Holy Spirit's enlightening and power. He gives the Bread of Life for the hungry and the Water of Life to all who thirst. There is also fire and warmth for those who have grown cold.

Practically it has been found best to arrange the chairs if possible in a circle, one of the group being chosen as leader, who will keep an eye on time. Punctual starting and ending is a good testimony to true caring one for another.

All those who come may ask themselves in prayer beforehand: Am I really wanting holiness and the fullness of the Spirit? Am I really willing to be open and to drop all masks? Am I willing to be challenged by the Holy Spirit, or by any member of the group? Am I willing in love to show up sin? This is the *Fellowship of the Holy Spirit* in action.

The place of meeting and the subject or passage can be announced before-hand, so that all can come prepared. Also the member of the group chosen as leader, who will have been notified beforehand, will sit in the circle among the others, who will assist with reading of a verse, or prayer, or testimony. There is no place in the Lord's sight for argument, controversy, or superiority, nor inferiority complex and shyness. Where there is freedom the Bible speaks, as we are not dealing with an ordinary book. "He who has an ear, let him hear what the Spirit says . . ." (Rev.2:7).

Unfortunately, there has grown up almost universally amongst Christians the idea that they must wait for a minister or other "expert" before they can understand the Bible. While gratefully acknowledging that the minister may be much used of God, and a valuable theologian, *to rely* on such a one is to fall into the gravest of errors. It is doubting the power of the Holy Spirit Himself to guide and to bestow His gifts, and forgetting that where two or three are gathered together Christ is there in the midst as He promised.

And lastly it must be remembered that the understanding of the Bible does not depend on man's mental attainments. The humblest brain may be wiser in the understanding of spiritual things than the greatest intellects of the world, if fully yielded to Christ.

ABBREVIATIONS

et al	and elsewhere; and others
ibid	in the same place
JBP	J. B. Phillips
KJV	King James Version (*or* Authorised Version—AV)
LXX	Septuagint (the Greek translation of the Old Testament)
NASB	New American Standard Bible
NBC	New Bible Commentary
NBD	New Bible Dictionary
NEB	New English Bible
TEV	To-day's English Version
RSV	*Note :* most quotations of Scripture are taken from the Revised Standard Version, by permission of the Division of Christian Education, National Council of Churches, U.S.A.

1: GOD—The Supreme Being

The Old Testament reveals a Supreme Being—the Eternal One, the "I AM", the Source of all Life. The plural noun "Elohim" signifies the transcendence and superlative character of the Godhead and anticipates the biblical truth of the Trinity. In the Old Testament, God reveals Himself and His character by His names, as meeting every human need. In the Unity of the Godhead there are Three Persons, Father, Son and Holy Spirit, which is what we mean by the word "Trinity". The Incarnation is foreshadowed by the Old Testament appearances of Christ.

ELOHIM = the All-Powerful One (plural). Used about 2,500 times in the Old Testament. Representing the Trinity—Father, Son and Holy Spirit.

>   Gen.1:1 et seq " .. In the beginning God .. " (Elohim)

EL (singular) = the Strong One, or the suggestion of "First Cause."

>   Ex.6:3 " .. as God Almighty .. "
>   2 Sam.22:33 " .. God is my strong refuge .. "

EL-ELYON = the Most High God, means Highest.

>   Gen.14:18–22 " .. priest of God Most High .. "

EL-SHADDAI = the All-Sufficient One (quoted Heb.7:1) the Satisfier, as a mother with a baby.

>   Gen.17:1 " .. I am God Almighty .. "
>   Gen.49:25 " .. who will bless you with blessings .. "
>   Gen.28:3, 4 " .. God Almighty .. make you fruitful .. "

EL-OLAM = the Everlasting God.

>   Gen.21:33 " .. the name of the Lord, the Everlasting God .. "

JEHOVAH (YAHWEH) = the Self-Existent One. The great I AM (used about 7,000 times). The personal name of the God of Israel, and the Redemptive name of God.

>   Ex.3:14 " .. God said, 'I AM WHO I AM' .. "
>   Ex.12:12, 13 " .. I am the Lord .. when I see the blood, I will pass over you .. "
>   Gen.3:21 " .. the Lord God made .. garments of skins .. "

JEHOVAH-ELOHIM = Lord God, as Creator.

>   Gen.1:26 " .. God said, 'Let us make man' .. "
>   Ex.3:6 " .. the God of Abraham .. Isaac .. Jacob .. "

JEHOVAH-JIREH = Jehovah will provide (a sacrifice).

>   Gen.22:13, 14 " .. a ram, caught in a thicket .. "

JEHOVAH-RAPHA = Jehovah that Healeth.

>   Ex.15:25 " .. the Lord shewed him a tree .. "
>   Ex.15:26 " .. I am the Lord, your healer .. "

JEHOVAH-NISSI = Jehovah is my Banner.

>   Ex.17:15 " .. Moses built an altar .. "

JEHOVAH-SHALOM = Jehovah is Peace.
Judges 6:24 " .. Gideon built an altar .. "
JEHOVAH-RAAH = Jehovah is my shepherd.
Ps.23:1 " .. The Lord is my shepherd .. "
JEHOVAH-TSIDKENU = Jehovah our Righteousness. A name for Messiah.
Jer.33:16 " .. Jerusalem .. will be called: 'The Lord is our righteousness' .. "
JEHOVAH-SHAMMAH = Jehovah is there.
Ezk. 48:35 " .. the name of the city .. The Lord is there .. "
JEHOVAH-SABAOTH = the Lord of Hosts. A manifestation of power revealed in time of need. Never mentioned in the books of Moses, but 88 times in Jeremiah in approaching judgement, and 14 times in two chapters of Haggai, and so on, in times of utmost extremity.
Ps.46:7, 11 " .. The Lord of hosts is with us .. "
Mal.3:17 " .. says the Lord of hosts .. I will spare them .. "
THE OMNIPOTENCE OF GOD = He cannot be overcome.
Jer.32:17 " .. Nothing is too hard for thee .. "
Matt.19:26 " .. with God all things are possible .. "
THE OMNIPRESENCE OF GOD = He cannot be avoided.
Ps.139:7-10 " .. whither shall I flee from they presence? .. "
Jer.23:24 " .. Can a man hide himself .. "
THE OMNISCIENCE OF GOD = He cannot be deceived.
Ps.139:1-6 " .. Thou .. art acquainted with all my ways .. "
Acts 15:18 " .. known from of old .. "
THE TRANSCENDENCE OF GOD = He cannot be excelled.
2 Chr.6:18 " .. the highest heaven cannot contain thee .. "
Is.66:1 " .. Heaven is my throne .. "
THE IMMUTABILITY OF GOD = He does not change.
Ps.102:26 " .. but thou dost endure .. "
James 1:17 " .. with whom there is no variation .. "
THE IMMANENCE OF GOD = He pervades everything, even every atom.
Prov.15:3 " .. The eyes of the Lord are in every place .. "
Matt.10:30 " .. even the hairs of your head .. "

GOD IS MERCIFUL   Ex.34:6 " .. merciful and gracious .. "
GOD IS HOLY   Lev.11:44 " .. I am the Lord .. I am holy .. "
                   John 17:11 Christ's prayer " .. Holy Father .. "
GOD IS SPIRIT   John 4:24 " .. God is spirit .. "
GOD IS LIGHT   1 John 1:5 " .. no darkness at all .. "
GOD IS LOVE   John 3:16 " .. For God so loved the world .. "
                   1 John 4:8 " .. God is love .. "

2: MAN—The Human Race

What is man? He was the last and greatest of God's creation, and was given a supreme place in the world. He was to possess the earth and to rule over it and all the animal kingdom. He was made "in the image of God", a noble and exalted figure in his original state. He is endowed with some of the attributes of God, such as wisdom, knowledge, love, goodness, free-will and power; but not omniscience, omnipresence or eternity. For this reason man is dependent on God, but the Bible tells us how he mis-used his independence.

In the Old Testament we find a detailed account of man's creation. He is tripartite—Spirit, Soul and Body. The spirit, Gr. "*pneuma*", is that part of man which "knows", i.e. is God-conscious. The soul, Gr. "*psyche*", implies the self-conscious life, the seat of the emotions, desires, affections and invididuality. The body, Gr. "*soma*", is that part which is world-conscious, which grows old and dies.

Gen.1:26 "..Let us make man.."
Gen.1:27 "..So God created man in his own image.."
Gen.2:7 "..and man becomes a living being.."
Gen.3:9 "..Where are you?.."
Prov.20:24 "..how then can man understand?.."
Zech.12:1 "..and formed the spirit of man within him.."
John 1:3 "..all things were made through him.."

Man is a special creation, inspired with the Breath of God, therefore the theory of mere evolution from a lower animal breaks down in his case. According to the Bible, Adam was an historical person. Man's sin and the need of atonement by Christ cannot be explained on any other basis apart from this view of his origin.

Gen.2:7 "..breathed..the breath of life.."
Job 33:4 "..the breath of the Almighty.."
Job 33:6 "..formed from a piece of clay.."
Gen.1:27 "..male and female he created them.."
Gen.5:2 "..he..named them Man.."
Acts 17:26 "..from one every nation of men.."
Matt.19:4 "..Jesus said, '..Have you not read?'.."
Mark 10:5, 6 "..Jesus said,..'God made them..'"

Man's fall and the two trees in the midst of the garden. Disobedience and the sin of doubt and lust came in and spoiled man's walk with God and caused him to be banished from the garden. Since then from every corner of the world has come the story of man's sin. Paul calls it the "carnal", "fleshly" or the Adamic nature of man, as opposed to the new nature after the New Birth. The "I" is in defeat till Christ comes.

Gen.3:1–6 "..Now the serpent was more subtle.."
Gen.2:9 "..the tree of life..the tree..of good and evil.."
Gen.6:5 "..The Lord saw..the wickedness of man.."
Rom.5:12 "..as sin came into the world through one man.."
Rom.7:23 "..in my members another law.."
1 Cor.3:1 "..as men of the flesh.."
2 Pet.1:4 "..in the world because of passion.."

In the New Testament, Jesus Christ, the "last Adam", the Perfect Man, is seen coming to the ruined world to bring back the likeness of God; and to bequeath new life to His followers who repent and are "born again" into His kingdom. (John 3:3). He came to seek and to save that which was lost.

Mark 8:36 ".. the whole world .."
Luke 15.3–7 .. The lost sheep.
Luke 15:11–24 .. The lost son.
Luke 15:8–10 .. The lost silver.
Rom.3:3 ".. Does their faithlessness ? .. "
Rom.5:12–21 ".. much more .. "
Rom.6:6 ".. old self .. crucified with him .. "
Eph.4:24 ".. and put on the new nature .. "
Col.1:15 ".. He is the image :. "
1 Thess.5:23 ".. your spirit and soul and body .. "

This, in outline, is the biblical Doctrine of Man.

3: SIN—Evil

What is Sin?
It is rebellion and enmity against God, demonstrated in a threefold-way: by act, by attitude, and by state; e.g. stealing is an *act* of sin, hypocrisy is an *attitude* of sin and being unsaved is a *state* of sin. Man therefore, by nature and in his triple state of body, soul and spirit, is in a condition of separation from God.

The origin of sin is revealed only in the Bible. The fact of sin in the world is undeniable. The dark stain of sin runs through the whole biblical revelation.

Gen.2:17 .. The fatal choice.
Gen.3:4-13, 18, 19 .. Adam and Eve hide.
Gen.13:13 .. Sin spreads.
Num.32:23 " .. your sin will find you out .. "
Ps.51:5 .. Born in sin.
Ps.66:18 " .. iniquity in my heart .. "
Prov.14:8 " .. the folly of fools .. "
Is.1:5, 6 " .. From the sole of the foot .. "
Ezek.18:4 " .. the soul that sins shall die .. "
Matt.5:21, 22 " .. angry with his brother .. "
Matt.5:27, 28 " .. looks .. lustfully .. "
Matt.23:28 " .. outwardly appear righteous .. "
Mark 7:20-23 .. Thirteen deadly sins.
Luke 18:11-14 .. The Pharisee and the publican.
John 16:8, 9 " .. he will convince the world of sin .. "
Rom.7:7-25 .. the "I" of self comes 32 times.
1 Cor.15:21, 22 " .. as by a man came death .. "
Gal.3:22 " .. consigned all things to sin .. "
Gal.5:19 " .. works of the flesh .. "
James 2:9 " .. if you show partiality .. "
James 4:17 " .. knows what is right .. "
1 John 1:8 " .. If we say .. no sin .. "
1 John 3:4, 8 " .. sin is lawlessness .. of the devil .. "

Sin is universal. By nature we are born in sin. Sin is a natural bias to which each man is ever prone, even those who have been regenerated. Sin is like a disease, an "infection of the nature", that must be washed away and even then, brought daily when necessary for renewed cleansing—(cf. John 13:10). Sin is like a burden on a man's back, which must be loosed from him, and buried. Christ alone was sinless.

Gen.3:8-10, 23, 24 " .. Where are you? .. "
Acts 17:26 " .. made from one every nation .. "
Rom.3:23 " .. all have sinned .. "
Rom.5:12 " .. through one man .. "
Rom.6:23 " .. the wages of sin .. "
Rom.7:24, 25 " .. Wretched man that I am! .. "
Eph.2:1-3 " .. children of wrath .. "
Heb.4:15 " .. tempted as we are .. "

1 Peter 2:22 " . . He committed no sin . . "
1 John 3:5 " . . to take away sins . . "

From the days of Adam, God had provided a remedy. The blood of the sacrificed animal made atonement for the man who offered it, if he truly repented and believed in its efficacy. But in the fullness of time, God came Himself, in the likeness of the Son of Man, the Lamb of God and voluntarily died once for all for the sin of the world. Since then belief in Him and in His blood shed for us, is the final and only way of escape from "the wages of sin (which) is death", i.e. eternal separation from God.

Gen.4:7 " . . sin is couching at the door . . "
Ex.12:21 " . . kill the passover lamb . . "
Is.1:13–18 " . . Come now, let us reason . . "
John 1:29 " . . Behold, the Lamb of God . . "
John 19:30 " . . It is finished . . "
Acts 4:12 " . . no other name under heaven . . "
Acts 13:38 " . . through this man forgiveness of sins . . "
Rom.5:19 " . . by one man's obedience . . "
Rom.6:11, 12 " . . Let not sin therefore reign . . "
Heb.9:26-28 " . . to put away sin . . "
1 John 1:7 " . . the blood of Jesus . . "
Rev.7:14 " . . These are they . . "

4: CHRIST—The Lord Jesus

The Anointed One, the official title of our Saviour, the Lord Jesus Christ. Since the fall of man, the coming of God to the world in an incarnate form was promised. He was to die vicariously for the world. Christ's official name in Hebrew was "Messiah"; in Greek, "Christos"; both mean "The Anointed One". His human name was in Hebrew, "Jehoshua", in Greek, "Jesus", and means "Saviour".

A chain of references runs through the Old Testament concerning Christ. Through Him all nations of the world were to be blessed.

Gen.3:15 " . . he shall bruise your head . . " The first promise of a Redeemer.
Gen.12:3 " . . I will bless . . you . . " (Abraham)
Gen.28:14 (Jacob) " . . by you and your descendants . . "
Is.9:6, 7 " . . to us a child is born . . "
Is.28:16 " . . precious cornerstone . . "
Is.42:1–3 (cf. Matt.12:18–21) " . . Behold my servant . . "
Zech.2:10-13 " . . Sing and rejoice . . "
Mal.3:1, 2 " . . Behold, I send my messenger . . "

Among the Jews, prophets, priests and kings were anointed—Christ was all three. He was to be anointed, not with oil, but with the Holy Spirit, and crowned, with thorns at the hands of men, and with glory at the hands of God.

Gen.49:10 " . . to whom it belongs . . "
Heb.4:14 (cf. Lev.8:12) " . . we have a great high priest . . "
Num.24:17 " . . a sceptre shall rise . . "
Deut.18:15, 18, 19 (cf. Acts 3:22, 23) " . . for you a prophet . . "
2 Sam.7:16 (cf. Luke 1:32, 33) " . . your kingdom shall be . . for ever . . "
Ps.110:1 Yahweh said " . . 'Sit at my right hand' . . "
Ps.110:4 (cf. Heb.5:6, 10) " . . a priest for ever . . "
Is.61:1, 2 (cf. Luke 4:18, 19) . . Christ quoted this of Himself.
Zech.9:9 " . . riding on an ass . . "
Heb.2:9 " . . crowned with glory and honour . . "

He was to be conceived miraculously of a virgin, and born at Bethlehem.

Is.7:13, 14 " . . a virgin shall conceive . . " (KJV)
Micah 5:2 " . . Bethlehem . . from you shall come forth . . "
Matt.1:23 " . . a virgin shall conceive . . "
Luke 1:35 " . . 'will be called holy' . . "

He was to suffer and die for the world, and it is implied that the "Suffering Servant" would rise again.

Ps.16:10 " . . to see corruption . . " (KJV)
Ps.22:1-18 (cf. Matt.27:46) " . . My God, my God, why hast thou . . "
Is.50:4-7 " . . my back to the smiters . . "
Is.52:13-15 " . . marred . . "
Is.53:1-12 " . . wounded for our transgressions . . "

Zech.11:10–13 (cf. Matt.27:9) ".. thirty pieces of silver.."
Zech.13:7 (cf. Matt.26:31) ".. 'Strike the shepherd'.."

In the New Testament the synoptists Matthew, Mark and Luke tell the story.

Matt.1:1, 23 ".. 'shall be called Emmanuel'.."
Matt.2:1–6 ".. born in Bethlehem.."
Matt.21:5 ".. mounted on an ass.."
Mark 15:18 ".. 'Hail, King of the Jews'.."
Luke 9:35 ".. 'This is my Son'.."
Matt.21:42 ".. 'which the builders rejected'.."
Matt.27:29 ".. a crown of thorns.."
Matt.27:35 ".. when they had crucified him.."
Matt.27:36 ".. they watched him there.." (KJV)

The Crucifixion. For six hours He hung on the cross, voluntarily dying for the failure of man. He was in unspeakable physical pain, but in a far more terrible way, He was in a position of temporary alienation from God as sin-bearer for us, a thing the human mind can never fully understand.

He looked out over the city that had cast Him out to die. The soldiers at His feet threw dice for His clothes—the priests exulted in their victory—the repentant robber prayed—the holiday crowd "looked on *Him there*". The world in type and reality was there before Him—the world for which He was dying. The greatest event in all history took place, on which all the past and future hang.

Mark 15:22–32 ".. 'He cannot save himself'.."
Luke 23:27–43 ".. Father, forgive them.."
John 12:32 ".. I, when I am lifted up.."
John 19:17–19 ".. Jesus between them.."
John 19:30 ".. 'It is finished'; and he bowed his head.."

Thus the great work of atonement was finished. Then the Lord Jesus rose from the grave, and was received back to heaven from whence He had come.

The Resurrection: The Easter miracle is at the heart of the Christian faith. It set the seal of God upon the sacrifice of Christ; it confirmed His Deity, and vindicated His promise that He would rise again. To-day it is experienced by believers in justification, Rom. 4:24, 25; in sanctification, Rom. 6:4; in power for living, Rom. 8:11, Phil. 3:10; and it is the assurance of their own resurrection-hope, 1 Cor. 15:12–19. See also study 39.

Note the indisputable proofs of Christ's resurrection.

1. The disappearance of the Lord's body. 2. The testimony of the apostles. 3. The existence of the Church. 4. The experience of countless people. 5. The clear Bible record. 6. The recurrence of revival in history.

The Bible is equally clear that He is to come back again; the next time as a King, in power and glory. This is the Second Coming; some feel that the signs of the times indicate that it is imminent.

Matt.28:6 ".. he has risen.."
Acts 1:9 ".. a cloud took him.."
Acts 1:11 He ".. will come in the same way.."

Other Biblical titles of Christ which reveal His character:

Matt.1:23 (Is.7:14) ".. Emmanuel .. God with us .. "
Is.9:6 ".. Wonderful Counsellor, Mighty God, Everlasting Father, Prince of Peace .. "
Dan.9:25 "Messiah"—Hebrew for "the anointed one", His official name.
Matt.1:1 ".. the son of David, the son of Abraham .. "
Matt.1:16 ".. Christ .. " = Greek "*Christos*".
Matt.3:3 et seq. ".. the Lord .. " = Greek "*kurios*" or master.
Matt.8:20 ".. the Son of man .. " This occurs 80 times in the New Testament. Cf. Dan.7:13.
Luke 1:32 ".. the Son of the most High .. " given by the angel Gabriel.
Luke 2:21 ".. Jesus .. " (Jehoshua in Hebrew) His human name.
Luke 4:3 ".. the Son of God .. " His divine title.
John 1:1, 14 ".. the Word .. " a concept of Him.
John 10:11 ".. the good shepherd .. "
John 14:6 ".. 'the way, and the truth, and the life' .. "
John 20:16 ".. 'Rabboni!' .. " My dear Master.
Phil.2:11 ".. Jesus Christ is Lord .. " This may mean Jehovah.
Rev.19:16 ".. KING OF KINGS AND LORD OF LORDS .. " (KJV)
Also many intimate metaphors are used to describe different aspects of His character—Bridegroom, Bread of Life, Water of Life, Advocate, Friend, *et al.*

N.B. The "Christophanies"—considered to be possible appearances of Christ, the pre-existent Son of God, in the Old Testament (see NBC, p.238 *et al.*):
Gen.16:7; 19:11; 22:48; 32:24. Ex.3:2; 14:19–22; 23:20; 32:34. Josh.5:13. Dan.3:25-28; 10:5–16. Hos.12:4. Zech.1:9 .

5: REPENTANCE—Change of heart

True repentance means a radical change of attitude towards God, and therefore towards sin. It is genuine sorrow for sin, accompanied by a change of heart (Gr. *metanoia* = a change of mind). It is an **attitude** of mind, as well as an act. Remorse, or doing penance, alone, is not real repentance.

Gen.27:38 (and Heb.12:17) .. Esau—tears only.
Matt.21:28-30 .. Words only—".. 'I go, sir,' but did not go.."
Matt.27:3-5 .. Judas. **Remorse** only.
2 Sam.12:13-18 David. ".. 'I have sinned'.."
Luke 15:17, 18,20 ".. 'Father, I have sinned'.." Real repentance.
Luke 15:7 ".. joy .. in heaven.."
Acts 8:21, 22, 24 ".. 'Pray for me'.." Simon the sorcerer trying to copy.

Repentance must precede the second birth, and it must be preached throughout the world. It is the key that unlocks the door to eternal life, by faith in Jesus Christ. Saving faith is impossible without repentance.

Matt.3:2, 8 .. John the Baptist's message.
Matt.4:17 ".. Jesus began to preach, saying, 'Repent'.."
Matt.9:13 ".. sinners to repentance.." (KJV)
Luke 24:47,48 ".. repentance and forgiveness of sins.."
Acts 2:38 ".. Peter said to them, 'repent'.."
Acts 17:30 ".. all men everywhere.."
Acts 20:21 ".. repentance to God and of faith.."
Acts 26:20 .. Paul's message, ".. repent and turn to God.."

Unwillingness to repent blinds and sears the conscience.

Matt.11:21 ".. Woe to you, Chorazin!.."
Is.1:13 ".. Bring no more vain oblations.."
Luke 13:3 ".. unless you repent.."
1 John 1:8 ".. if we say we have no sin.."
Heb.6:6 ".. if they then commit apostasy.."

The attitude of repentance: "brokenness", the broken "and contrite heart" (Heb. *shabar* = shivered or shattered.) The same complete surrender and yielding that took place when we first came to Christ, must persist in life and *become a habit and an attitude of mind* in our walk with God. Every challenge and warning of the Holy Spirit must be instantly accepted, and even welcomed. This is the secret of **holiness**, and of **revival**:—"Break me! Melt me! Mould me! Fill me!"

Ps.51:17 ".. a broken and contrite heart, O God.."
Ps.147:3 ".. He heals the brokenhearted.."
Is.61:1 ".. to bind up the brokenhearted.."
Jer.23:9 ".. My heart is broken within me.."
2 Chr.7:14 ".. if my people .. humble themselves.."
Luke 4:18 ".. He hath sent me to heal the brokenhearted.." (KJV)
(the first five use the Heb. "*shabar*")

God repeatedly *warns the unrepentant man*—but His arms are always outstretched to receive.

Ezek.18 " . . 'I have no pleasure in the death of anyone,' says the Lord . . "

Is.65:2 " . . I spread out my hands all the day . . "

Luke 15:20 " . . his father . . ran . . and kissed him . . "

Rom.10:21 " . . 'All day long I have held out my hands to a disobedient . . people' . . "

2 Pet.3:9 " . . not wishing that any should perish . . "

Rev.3:19 " . . whom I love, I reprove and chasten; so . . repent . . "

"Conviction of sin is one of the rarest things a man ever strikes. It is the first threshold of getting to understand God." *Oswald Chambers.*

6: REPENTANCE—Confession of sin

There are two types of confession, a statement or confession of one's faith, or the confession of one's sin and guilt. In the Bible confession of sin before God is recognised as a condition of forgiveness. It is always an accompaniment of revival when the Holy Spirit brings conviction of sin. Nothing can stop convicted men and women from making a "clean breast" of hidden sin. Great care needs to be taken in attempting to direct or check the movings of the Spirit. Finney says that "the spontaneous open confession of hidden sin to the Lord has always been an accompaniment of revival, and it is the floodgates which, when opened, let the blessings flow in."

God requires confession of sin, not necessarily public.

Lev.5:5 ".. When a man is guilty .. he shall confess the sin .. "
Prov.28:13 ".. He who conceals .. he who confesses .. "
Matt.3:6 ".. confessing their sins .. "
Rom.10:9 ".. confess with your lips .. "

Confession is essentially to God, and to Christ as Sinbearer.

Lev.16:21 ".. confess over him (the goat) all the iniquities .. "
Ps.32:5 ".. 'I will confess .. to the Lord' .. "
Ps.51:4 ".. Against thee .. have I sinned .. "
Ps.51:17 ".. a broken and contrite heart .. "
Luke 15:18 ".. 'Father I have sinned' .. "

Victory and revival are held up by hidden sin. Joshua pleads with Achan to reveal his sin. Defeat was inevitable till confession was made. So it will ever be with the church of God.

Josh.7:19 ".. tell me now .. do not hide it .. "

Confession to one another and reconciliation.

Num.5:6, 7 ".. he shall confess .. and .. make .. restitution .. "
Matt.5:23, 24 ".. your brother has something against you .. first be reconciled .. "
Matt.18:15 ".. 'If your brother sins against you .. ' .. "
Matt.18:22 .. How many times? ".. 'seventy times seven' .. "

Confession to the assembly. Such a confession, when made, should be primarily to God, in the hearing of the assembly. It is especially appropriate when the fault has been well-known and when it has been a stumbling-block to others, or a public scandal reflecting upon the testimony of the local church.

Josh.7:20 ".. And Achan answered Joshua, ' .. I have sinned .. and this is what I did ' .. "
Ezra 10:1 ".. While Ezra prayed and made confession, weeping .. "

Confession with wrong motives.

Since open confession is often necessary *Satan does not let it pass unchallenged.* Confession is wrong if the person thinks:

1.—that public confession in itself takes away sin, and trusts in *it* instead of in the cleansing power of the blood of Christ.
2.—that by doing it he will get the praise of men.

3.—that he must do it because it is the custom of his church.
4.—that it will bring attention to himself.
5. that he will be put out of fellowship if he does not do it.
6.—that he has freedom to speak of things of shame.
Eph.5:12 " . . it is a shame even to speak . . "

Confession may be hindered by fear of man.
John 12:42 " . . for fear . . they did not confess . . "

7: FAITH—Trust in Jesus

Faith may be described as complete and unreserved trust in God as the fulfiller of His promises contained in His Word, and in Jesus Christ as Saviour and Lord. Thus Christ is the object of this faith. He is the "pioneer and perfecter of our faith". (Heb.12:2.) The "redeemed" walk the road of faith. (Is.35:9.) The fundamental basis of true faith is redemption. The Hebrew word *aman* is generally used in the Old Testament and is translated by "believe". This special faith may be called **Redemptive Faith.**

In Old Testament times it appears that all those who saw in faith, behind the blood of their sacrifices, their redemption, *experienced* forgiveness, after truly repenting.

Gen.4:4 .. Abel's faith. cf. Heb.11:4 and 1 John 3:12.
Gen.5:24 .. Enoch's faith. cf. Heb.11:5.
Gen.8:20 .. The faith of Noah. cf. Heb.11:7.
Gen.15:6 .. Abraham's faith. cf. Heb.11:8.
Ex.12:21-25 .. The Passover of Moses. cf. Heb.11:28.
Josh.6:20 .. Joshua's faith at Jericho.cf. Heb.11:30.
Ps.2:12 ⎱.. The word 'trust' used for faith but the same word in
Ps.37:3 ⎰ Greek—*pisteuo*.
Hab.2:4 " .. shall live by his faith .. "

In the New Testament Christ claimed to fulfil the Old Testament promises, and hence faith was to be in Him from that time onwards. John the Baptist was the first to call, "Behold the Lamb of God!" John 1:29.

Matt.8:10 " .. such faith .. "
Matt.9:22 " .. your faith has made you well .. "
Matt.17:20 " .. as a grain of mustard seed .. "
Mark 9:23 " .. If thou canst **believe** .. " (another English word for faith, and the same word in Greek). (KJV)
Luke 22:32 " .. that your faith may not fail .. "
Luke 24:27 " .. the things concerning himself .. "
John 3:16 " .. whoever believes in him .. "
John 7:38 " .. believes in me .. rivers .. "
John 8:24 " .. die in your sins .. "
John 12:46 " .. whoever believes .. "

The Apostles went out into the world with this one message, "**Believe** in the Lord Jesus Christ." Christians came to be called "believers."

Acts.3:16 " .. by faith in his name .. "
Acts 10:43 " .. who believes in him .. "
Rom.3:24 " .. redemption .. in Christ Jesus .. "
Rom.5:1 " .. justified by faith .. "
Rom.10:4 " .. Christ .. the end of the struggle .. " (JBP)
Rom.10:10 " .. confesses with his lips .. "
1 Cor.2:2 " .. Christ and him crucified .. "
Gal.2:20 " .. I live by faith .. "
Eph.6:16 " .. the shield of faith .. "

1 Tim.6:12 " . . the good fight of the faith . . "
1 Pet.2:7 . . Precious faith!

Other aspects of Faith.

(a) **The Prayer of Faith.** James 5:14, 15. " . . the prayer of faith will save the sick man . . "—Countless Christians have prayed this prayer over a sick or suffering one, sometimes with the anointing of oil and laying on of hands, and in the presence of praying friends. The true prayer of faith is operative when we all know for a *certainty* that God can cure, even instantly, *if He so wills*. Confusion and disappointment arise when those praying *dictate* to God. It is not always His will to cure, as with Paul's "thorn in the flesh".

(b) **Faith-Healing, a Gift of the Spirit.** It may be that God is reviving this gift of healing in these last days.
Gal.5:22. There are nine **fruits** of the Spirit—" . . love, joy, peace . . ", etc. of which **faithfulness** is one.
1 Cor.12:9. There are nine **gifts** of the Spirit of which **faith** is one.

(c) **Living by Faith.** 1 Cor.9:14. " . . those who proclaim the gospel should get their living by the gospel . . ". This is generally taken to mean that those living this way are trusting God for all their material necessities, relying entirely on Him to provide for His servant.

(d) **Overcoming Faith.** 1 John 5:4. " . . this is the victory that overcomes the world, our faith . . ". There are times, especially in revival, when faith is so strong that the conviction becomes sure, that God is going to do a certain thing. This is sometimes referred to as "praying through". "This power is victoriously operative only in believers." (NBC)

The Biblical Summary: Heb.11:1-39;12:1, 2 " . . a cloud of witnesses . . " who lived and died by faith, and pre-eminently Jesus who is the "pioneer and perfecter of our faith."

8: ATONEMENT—at-one-ment

Atonement is an English composite word meaning **Reconciliation**: i.e. **at-one-ment**. The word atonement translates in the Old Testament the Hebrew word *Kaphar*, to cover, meaning thereby that sins were covered by the blood of the sacrifice, and that the sinner and God had become "at one". But now in theology, the word atonement has come to include the whole theme of redemption through the Blood of Christ. The word does occur once in the New Testament, where it is used for reconciliation, in Romans 5:11. (KJV)

In Old Testament times sins were covered by God in anticipation of the Cross. A man having truly repented, sacrificed his innocent animal, and trusted that God would fulfil His promise of cleansing him from his sin, if he offered the blood of the sacrifice.

Ex.30:10, 16 " . . to make atonement . . "
Lev.1:3, 4 " . . lay his hand upon the head . . "

Examples of *Kaphar* used as "Reconciliation".

Lev.8:15 " . . reconciliation . . " *(kaphar)* for the priests . . (KJV)
Ezk.45:15 " . . reconciliation . . " for the princes and rulers (KJV);
   no dishonesty, corruption, oppression, violence, debts, or
   altering of weights and measures.
Ezk.45:17 " . . for the house of Israel . . "
Dan.9:24 " . . to finish the transgression . . "

The Day of Atonement (Lev.16) the tenth day of the seventh month, (September) was Israel's most solemn holy day, a day of humiliation. No work was allowed, and a strict fast enjoined. The High Priest, after ceremonial cleansing, took the blood of the sacrificial animal into the Holy of Holies to make atonement for the sins of the people. Then after confessing their sins with his hands on the head of a second goat—the scapegoat—he handed it over to be led out into the wilderness and set free, symbolizing the carrying away of their sins.

The Day of Atonement is still observed by Jews all over the world up to the present time; " . . the sacrificial aspects . . have not been in effect since the destruction of the Temple . ." (NBD, p.111).

Lev.16:11, 17, 30 . . Aaron's atonement.
Lev.17:11 " . . the blood that makes atonement . . "
Lev.23:27 " . . the day of atonement . . "
Animal sacrifices were the shadows of which the death of Christ became the reality.

John 1:29 " . . 'Behold, the Lamb of God!' . . "
Rom.3:25   } . . a "propitiation" i.e. it makes us what we could
1 John 4:10 }   not otherwise be—acceptable to God (KJV)
Heb.9:13–15, 22, 26 " . . how much more . ."
Heb.10:1, 4 " . . a shadow of the good things to come . . "
1 John 2:2 " . . the sins of the whole world . . "

And now **under grace**, having repented of our sins, and having put our faith in Christ who died for us, the righteous (One) for the unrighteous (ones), to bring us to God, we are in fact reconciled to God. Atonement has been made. His shed blood was the price paid for the redemption of the world. His death was the supreme event in the history of the world.

Mark 10:45 " . . a ransom for many . . "
John 10:11 " . . his life for the sheep . . "
Rom.3:21-25 " . . justified by his grace . . "
Rom.5:10, 11, 19 . . His death was "representative"
2 Cor.5:21 " . . made him to be sin . . "
Eph.1:7 " . . redemption . . "
1 Peter 1:18, 19 " . . with the precious blood . . "
1 Peter 2:24 . . His death was "vicarious" (or "substitutionary")
1 Peter 3:18 " . . Christ . . died for sins . . "

Isaac Watt's hymn immortalises this theme:—

My faith would lay her hand
On that dear head of Thine,
While like a pentitent I stand,
And there confess my sin.

Terms used for the Atonement:

Representative:—representing sinful men.
Propitiatory:—making sinful men acceptable to a holy God.
Vicarious:—dying in the place of sinful men.

9: SACRIFICE—Dying for the human race

Sacrifice in its original sense implied the offering of an innocent animal for the guilt of the individual. Where this was accompanied by true repentance and faith, God looked upon the shed blood and granted atonement in anticipation of the Cross.

In the Old Testament it is assumed that God must have initiated man, His special creation, into the meaning of sacrifice. The ".. garments of skins .." (Gen.3:21) came from slain animals. Man was created to walk with God, so after sin came in the only way back was shown to be through repentance and the vicarious sacrifice of an animal. Anthropologists and archaeologists find traces of this practice in all parts of the world, going back to the earliest times.

>   Gen.4:3 .. Abel seemed to know the right way.
>   Gen.7:1 and 8:20 ".. Noah built an altar .. "
>   Gen.22:8, 13 .. The ram in the thicket.
>   Gen.31:54 ".. Jacob offered a sacrifice .. "
>   Ex.12:3 ".. every man a lamb .. "
>   Ex.18:12 .. and Jethro likewise.
>   Lev.1:2, 3, 4 ".. to make atonement for him .. "
>   1 Sam.15:22 ".. better than sacrifice .. "
>   Is.1:13 ".. vain offerings .. "
>   Heb.10:1 ".. the law .. a shadow of the good things to come .. "

True sacrifice, as ordained by God in the Old Testament, was the shadow of which Christ's death was the reality. But Cain's offering which God rejected may have been the forerunner of the almost all universal perversion of sacrifice, leading to idolatry and immorality.

Two things were necessary for Atonement in the O.T.

>   a. Repentance .. Num.5:7 ".. he shall confess his sin .. "
>   b. Faith in the blood of the sacrifice .. Lev.17:11 ".. the blood
>   .. to make atonement for your souls .. "

N.B. An important part of the sacrificial system was ceremonial washing, which typifies the necessity of cleansing from the defilement of sin (death, leprosy), just as Christian baptism is an outward and visible sign of the cleansing and renewing effect of the atoning work of Christ in the heart and life of the believer. Ex.40:32 ".. they washed ..," Num.8:7, 21, ".. sprinkle the water .."

The New Testament period opens with John the Baptist's triumphant cry: "Behold the Lamb of God .. ". The Bible ends in the book of Revelation with the glory of Him who was "slain from the foundation of the world."

>   Matt.1:21 ".. save his people from their sins .. "
>   John 1:36 ".. Behold, the Lamb of God! .. "
>   John 3:16 ".. God so loved the world .. "
>   1 Cor.5:7 ".. Christ our passover .. " (KJV)
>   Heb.9:13, 14 ".. how much more .. "
>   1 Pet.1:18, 19 ".. with the precious blood .. "
>   Rev.13:8 ".. from the foundation of the world .. " (KJV)

The Sacrifice of Christ for the sin of the world was final. There is no other way, and no other Gospel. The veil of the Jewish Temple was torn in two at the death of Christ, thus destroying in type the old barrier between sinful man and a holy God. Therefore from the earliest times true Christians have scorned the continued offering of animals or things, accepting only as of value to Christ the offering of their spiritual sacrifices of prayer, praise, thanksgiving, and of a humble and contrite heart. As there are no more atoning sacrifices, there is no more need of a priest (*Sacerdos*).

John 10:18 " . . I lay it down . . "
John 12:32, 33 " . . I, when I am lifted up . . "
John 17:4 " . . having accomplished the work . . "
John 19:30 " . . It is finished . . "
Rom.3:25 . . A propitiatory sacrifice, i.e. an appeasement.
Rom.5:9 " . . much more shall we . . "
I Cor.6:20 " . . bought with a price . . "
2 Cor.5:19 " . . not counting their trespasses . . "
Gal.3:13 " . . become a curse . . "
Eph.1:7 " . . the forgiveness of sins . . " (KJV)
Col.1:21, 22 " . . he has now reconciled . . "
Heb.9:12 " . . eternal redemption . . "
Heb.10:10–18 " . . sat down at the right hand of God . . "
Rev.7:17 " . . the Lamb in the midst of the throne . . "
Rev.21:23 " . . the Lamb is the light thereof . . " (KJV)
   —Heaven rings with praise of the Lamb.

Two things are necessary for atonement in the N.T.
   a. Repentance . . Acts 20:21 " . . repentance to God . . "
   b. Faith in the blood of Christ . . Rom.3:24, 25 " . . an expiation
      by his blood, to be received by faith . . "

N.B. Christian Baptism is a public testimony before others, of the salvation (atonement) that the person has claimed in his heart by faith. Acts 8:36 . . "See, here is water! . . "

10: REDEMPTION—Buying back

The word redemption can be explained simply in two ways, (a) the setting at liberty of a prisoner by paying his ransom in full; (b) the buying back of something that has been sold by paying the full price. When used spiritually in this way, it means the delivering of a sinner from the bondage of Satan, sin, and death, by the precious blood of Christ, which is the ransom price. He is Redeemer and Ransom combined.

In the Old Testament the Kinsman-Redeemer (Heb. *Go'el*) is a beautiful picture of Christ our Redeemer. There were two essentials. He had to be a kinsman, and he had to be able to pay the full price.

Lev.25:25, 26 " . . to redeem it . . "
Lev.25:48, 49 " . . near kinsman . . "
Ruth 3:12, 13 ⎱ . . Christ (the Bethlehemite) redeems the Church
Ruth 4:4–6 ⎰ (Ruth) a Gentile.
Job 19:25 " . . my Redeemer lives . . "
Ps.19:14 " . . my strength and my redeemer . . " (KJV)
Is.59:20 " . . to Zion as Redeemer . . "

Redemption in the New Testament fulfils the Old Testament types, but three Greek words are used and translated as Redemption:

(a) *agorazo* = "to purchase IN the (slave) market."
(b) *exagorazo* = "to buy OUT OF the (slave) market."
(c) *lutroo* = "to pay the ransom for", and so "to redeem from death or from slavery."

Mark 10:45 " . . a ransom for many . . "
Luke 1:68 " . . redeemed his people . . "
Acts 20:28 " . . obtained with his own blood . . "
Rom.7:14 " . . sold under sin . . "
Rom.8:2 " . . set me free . . "
1 Cor.1:30 " . . and redemption . . "
Gal.4:4, 5 " . . adoption of sons . . "
Eph.1:7, 14 " . . we have redemption . . "
1 Tim.2:6 " . . a ransom for all . . "
Titus 2:14 " . . a people of his own . . "

The purchase price is not "silver or gold", but the blood of the Redeemer, shed for us on Calvary. We are redeemed from the guilt, the penalty, and the dominion of sin.

Ps.49:15 " . . from the power of the grave . . " (KJV)
Luke 21:28 " . . your redemption is drawing near . . "
Gal.3:13 " . . from the curse of the law . . "
1 Pet.1:18, 19 " . . as silver or gold . . "
Rev.5:9 " . . from every . . nation . . "
Rev.14:4 " . . these have been redeemed . . "

11: JUSTIFICATION—Acquittal

What is meant by Justification? It is the same as righteousness. The Greek adjective *dikaios* is often translated "righteous", and the verb *dikaioo* as "to justify". It is a judicial acquittal. It is "the accounting as righteous" of a believer. It is a free gift from God—the God against whom we have sinned. It is the Judge Himself who makes the declaration. The justified believer has been in court, only to learn that nothing is laid to his charge.

In the Old Testament "righteous" and "just" are English words used to translate the Hebrew *tsadiq*, "just", and *tsidqah*, "righteousness", both meaning to be right with God, that is to say, not sinless, but one who offered in faith the required sacrifice.

Lev.4:27–35 " . . lay his hand on the head of the sin offering . . "
Eccl.7:20 " . . not a righteous man on earth . . "
Is.50:8 " . . he who vindicates me . . "

In the New Testament we are justified because Christ has borne our sins on the Cross. God, as Judge, declares that those who believe in Christ as Saviour are justified and righteous.

John.5:24 " . . he does not come into judgement . . "
Rom.3:19, 20, 24–26 " . . they are justified by his grace . . "
Rom.4:5, 8 " . . will not reckon his sin . . "
Rom.5:1, 9 " . . justified by faith . . "
Rom.8:1, 31–34 " . . no condemnation . . "
1 Cor.1:30 " . . God made . . our righteousness . . "
2 Cor.5:21 " . . made him to be sin . . "

Justification is entirely a work of grace, i.e. it is unmerited, and "not by works of righteousness which we have done." Good works, pleading, self-sacrifice, giving all one's goods, are unavailing.

Rom.3:24, 28–30 " . . by his grace as a gift . . "
Rom.5:16–18 " . . for all men . . "
Gal. 2:16 " . . not . . by works of the law . . "
Gal.3:8, 11, 24 " . . the law . . our schoolmaster . . " (KJV)
Gal.5:4 " . . fallen away from grace . . "

Man must admit his guilt before the all-righteous Judge and then he is justified by faith. Afterwards the life must bear witness to the faith.

Titus 3:1, 2 " . . be obedient . . honest . . "
James 2:24 " . . works . . faith . . "

This great doctrine of Justification by Faith had its re-birth at the time of the Reformation. Luther called it "the doctrine of a standing or a falling church."

12: THE GOSPEL—Good News

The word "gospel" means "good tidings". It comes from two Anglo-Saxon words: "god" = good, and "spell" = News. The Greek word *evangelion* really means "good message", and is translated "gospel" in the New Testament.

The gospel is the good message entrusted to Christ's followers to tell the world that salvation is to be had. It offers this salvation, and shows how it is obtained.

In the Old Testament a chain of promises can be traced relating to the coming of Christ and His Kingdom. But He was to be a suffering Messiah.

Gen.3:15 ".. bruise his heel .. "
Gen.12:3 ".. of the earth be blessed .. " (KJV; cf. Gal.3:8)
Is.41:27 ".. a herald of good tidings .. "
Is.52:7 ".. beautiful upon the mountains .. "
Is.53:3 et seq. ".. man of sorrows .. "
Is.61:1 ".. to preach good tidings .. " (KJV)

In the New Testament the gospel is revealed. "The heart of the gospel is that God himself meets this frightful deadlock (of man's sin) by a personal visit to the world" (J. B. Phillips.) Jesus goes about preaching and healing.

Mark 1:1 ".. the gospel of Jesus Christ .. "
Mark 1:4, 7 .. John the Baptist's gospel.
Mark 1:14 ".. Jesus .. preaching the gospel .. "
Mark 8:35 .. The gospel of Jesus.
Mark 10:29 ".. for my sake, and the gospel's .. " (KJV)
Mark 16:15 ".. Go ye into all the world .. " (KJV)
Luke 2:10 ".. good news of a great joy .. "
Luke 4:18 ".. to preach good news to the poor .. "
Luke 24:47 ".. beginning from Jerusalem .. "

Christ said that immediately after His death the Holy Spirit would take His place and guide His followers, who were commissioned to proclaim the enlarged message of the Gospel of Grace to the ends of the earth.

Matt.24:14 ".. then the end will come .. "
Mark 13:10 ".. must first be preached .. "
John 14:26 ".. the Comforter .. shall teach you .. " (KJV)
John 15:26 ".. bear witness .. "
John 16:8 ".. he will convince the world .. "
Acts 8:4, 5 ".. preaching the word .. "
Acts 14:21 .. Paul and Barnabas ".. preached the gospel .. "
Acts 15:7 ".. the Gentiles .. hear .. the gospel .. "
Acts 16:10 ".. into Macedonia .. " (Europe)
Acts 20:24 ".. accomplish my course .. "
Rom.1:1 ".. for the gospel of God .. "
Rom.1:15 ".. also .. in Rome .. "
Rom.10:15 ".. the gospel of peace .. " (KJV)
Rom.16:25 ".. kept secret .. "

1 Cor.1:17 " . . not with eloquent wisdom . . "
1 Cor.4:15 " . . your father . . through the gospel . . "
2 Cor.4:4 " . . the gospel of the glory . . "
2 Cor.10:16 " . . in lands beyond you . . "
Eph.3:8 " . . unsearchable riches . . "

There are two warnings. Firstly, Paul says that anyone, even "an angel out of heaven", who preaches "any other gospel" is accursed, "*anathema*". Secondly, God does not guarantee that the true gospel will always carry all before it, some will always reject it, and there will be persecution.

Matt.13:15 " . . ears . . heavy . . eyes . . closed . . "
Acts 13:50 " . . and stirred up persecution . . "
Acts 14:22 " . . through many tribulations . . "
2 Cor.4:3, 4 " . . if our gospel is veiled . . "
2 Cor.11:1-4, 13-15 " . . will be led astray . . "
Gal.1:6 " . . a different gospel . . "
Gal.1:8 " . . let him be accursed . . "
Gal.2:14 " . . were not straightforward . . "
Gal.4:13 . . Paul preached in weakness.
Phil.1:5 " . . partnership in the gospel . . "
Phil.1:16 " . . defence of the gospel . . "
Phil.1:27 " . . striving . . for . . the gospel . . "
Col.1:23 " . . stable and steadfast . . "
1 Thes.1:5 " . . in power and in the Holy Spirit . . "
1 Thes.2:2 " . . shamefully treated . . "
1 Thes.2:9 " . . worked night and day . . "
2 Tim.1:8 " . . suffering for the gospel . . "
Philemon 13 " . . during my imprisonment . . "
Jude 3 " . . contend for the faith . . "
Rev.14:6 " . . an eternal gospel . . "

Paul says: "Woe to me if I do not preach the gospel!" 1 Cor.9:16.

13: FORGIVENESS—Set free

The fundamental meaning of forgiveness in Scripture is—the separation of the sinner from his sin, as a man relieved of a load that he had been carrying. Human forgiveness means the remission of penalty, divine forgiveness is a complete exoneration. The Hebrew word, *kaphar* = cover, is connected with sacrifice and carries a sense of atonement and of forgiveness.

In the Old Testament the divine forgiveness follows the execution of the penalty . . "The priest shall make an atonement . . for his sin that he hath sinned, and it shall be forgiven him." Faced with the sacrifice, and recognising the value of it, the repentant sinner was forgiven.

Ex.34:7, 8 . . Forgiveness granted at Sinai.
Lev.4:20, 26 " . . they shall be forgiven . . "
Lev.5:10, 18 " . . he shall be forgiven . . "
Num.15:25, 26 " . . because it was an error . . "
Ps.32:5 " . . thou didst forgive . . my sin . . "
Ps.85:2 " . . Thou didst forgive . . thy people . . "
Ps.103:12 " . . as far as the east is from the west . . "
Is.38:17 " . . all my sins behind thy back . . "
Jer.31:34 " . . remember their sin no more . . "
Is.44:22 " . . I have swept away . . "
Dan.9:9, 19 . . Daniel's cry for forgiveness.

In the New Testament the divine forgiveness is announced in the words " . . this is my blood of the covenant, which is poured out for many for the forgiveness of sins" (Matt.26:28, KJV). Any sinner in any place at any time of day or night can approach God, and receive (experience) forgiveness, on the ground of **Christ's propitiatory sacrifice.**

Matt.6:12 . . The Lord's prayer.
Mark 2:5 " . . your sins are forgiven . . "
Luke 7:49 " . . 'Who is this, who . . forgives sins?' . . "
Matt.26:28 " . . for the forgiveness of sins . . "
Luke 17:3, 4 " . . seven times in the day . . "
Luke 23:34 " . . 'Father, forgive them . . ' . . "
Acts 13:38 " . . forgiveness of sins . . "
Rom.4:7 " . . Blessed are those . . "
2 Cor.2:7–10 . . Paul's forgiveness.
Eph.1.7 " . . through his blood . . "
Col.2:13 " . . forgiven us all our trespasses . . "
Heb.9:22 " . . without the shedding of blood there is no forgiveness . . "
Acts 7:60 . . Stephen's forgiveness.

Warnings.
(a) Matt.6:15 " . . if you do not forgive . . "
(b) Ps.66:18 " . . If I had cherished iniquity . . "
(c) Matt.12:31, 32 " . . blasphemy . . "

How many times do I have to forgive my brother? The Bible is very clear.

Matt.5:23, 24 " . . your brother has something against you . . "
Matt.18:15 " . . If your brothers sins against you . . "
Matt.18:21, 22 " . . but seventy times seven . . "
Luke 17:3, 4 " . . seven times in the day . . "
Luke 19:8 " . . I restore it fourfold . . "
Eph.4:32 " . . forgiving one another . . "
Col.3:13 . . make a habit of forgiving.
James 5:15 " . . the prayer of faith . . "
1 John 1:9 " . . will forgive our sins . . "

The greatest forgiveness of all times, from the Cross.
Luke 23:34 " . . 'Father, forgive them . . ' . . "

14: ETERNAL LIFE—Lasting for ever

It is generally agreed that the Bible teaches that there is inevitably for each man an immortality, which will be Eternal Life, or Eternal Death (i.e. eternal separation from God). On being born again we become partakers of Life Eternal. God is eternal; He is the "I AM, who was, and is, and is to come," but as a result of the fall we can have Eternal Life only on God's terms.

In the Old Testament we find God as the God of Eternity, " .. from everlasting to everlasting", and every page points forward to the coming of Christ, who is Eternal Life. Enoch, Noah, Abraham, Moses, David and Elijah and countless others entered into that eternal life by faith.

Gen.5:24 and 6:9 .. Enoch and Noah "walked with God .. "
Gen.21:33 .. El Olam, " .. the everlasting God .. "
Ex.3:6 " .. the God of .. Abraham .. Isaac, and .. Jacob .. "
Ex.15:18 " .. will reign for ever .. "
Deut.33:27 " .. The eternal God .. "
Ps.73:24 " .. afterward thou wilt receive me to glory .. "
Is.57:15 " .. who inhabits eternity .. "
Jer.10:10 " .. the Lord .. the everlasting King .. "
Micah 5:2 .. Christ " .. from of old .. "
Habak.1:12 " .. from everlasting .. We shall not die .. "

In the New Testament Christ came to reveal Eternal Life, and to give it freely to all who believe in Him.

Matt.7:13, 14 " .. the narrow gate .. leads to life .. "
Matt.19:16 " .. to have eternal life? .. "
Matt.25:46 " .. into eternal life .. "
John 3:15 " .. have eternal life .. "

Eternal Life is imparted to every true believer at the New Birth.

John 6:27, 40 " .. to everlasting life .. " (KJV)
John 8:12 " .. the light of life .. "
John 10:10 " .. life .. abundantly .. "
John 10:28 " .. shall never perish .. "
John 11:25 " .. yet shall he live .. "
John 14:6 " .. 'I am .. the life .. ' .. "
John 17:3 " .. eternal life .. Jesus .. "
John 20:31 " .. life in his name .. "

Christ is called in Scripture: "The Prince of Life" Acts 3:15 (KJV).
Acts 13:46 .. Eternal life goes to the Gentiles.
Rom.6:23 " .. the free gift of God .. "
2 Cor.5:4 .. Death has no horrors.
Phil.2:16 " .. the word of life .. "
Col.3:3 " .. hid with Christ .. "
Col.3:4 " .. with him in glory .. "
1 Tim.6:12 " .. take hold of the eternal life .. "
2 Tim.1:10 " .. Christ .. brought .. immortality .. "
James1:12 " .. the crown of life .. "
1 John 1.1 " .. the word of life .. "

Rev.2:7 " . . the **tree** of life . . "
Rev.21:6 " . . the **water** of life . . "
Rev.22:19 " . . the book of life . . " (KJV)

The names of believers are written in the Lamb's Book of Life. Rev.21:27.

15: THE KINGDOM OF HEAVEN—The Kingdom of God

This is one of the central themes of the Bible. It is synonymous with the Kingdom of God. It was God's plan for man to have dominion over creation in an earthly Paradise, where, perhaps, longevity was to be increased and ferocity absent from the animal world. But in some way, revealed only in the Bible, sin entered in, and the Kingdom came back only through Christ the Incarnate God, coming into the world and dying on the cross to break the power of evil and win men back to God.

In the Old Testament God's plan of coming to dwell among men is unfolded, and the way is prepared for His spiritual Kingdom.

Gen.1:26 " . . dominion over . . fish . . birds . . cattle . . "
Gen.3:5, 6 . . Envy,—"lust-for-more" crept in.
Ex.3:7 " . . the Lord . . heard their cry . . "
Ex.19:9 . . He came down to Sinai.
Ex.24:12 . . The laws of the Kingdom are given.
Ex.25:22 . . God comes lower, to the Mercy Seat.
Deut.30:1–9 . . Blessings and cursings, "Yes" or "No".
1 Sam.9:17 . . Saul made King.
1 Sam.16:13 . . David anointed.
2 Kings 25:7 . . Final deportation.
Ps.2:1–9 . . A King predicted.
Is.7:14 " . . a virgin shall conceive . . " (KJV)
Is.9:6 " . . Prince of Peace . . "
Is.11:6 " . . The wolf . . shall dwell with the lamb . . "

The near and a far view of a coming Kingdom in the prophetic books. The near view was Sennacherib's invasion, the far view is the Day of the Lord.

Is.32:1, 2, 14–18 . . Sennacherib's invasion near.
Is.35:1–10 . . The Highway of Holiness, near and far view.
Jer.23:5 " . . a righteous Branch . . "

The near and far promise of the Jews' return to the land—*first* temporary after seventy years of exile, the *second* will be the final restoration of the Davidic Kingdom, when all earthly rulers will bow before the " . . stone . . cut out without hands . . "

Jer.29:10 . . (after seventy years) " . . I will visit you . . "
Ezk.34:11 " . . I . . will search for my sheep . . "
Ezk.37:22 " . . I will make them one nation . . "
Dan.2:34 " . . a stone . . cut out by no human hand . . "
Dan.7:13 " . . came with the clouds . . " (KJV)
Is.11:11 " . . the second time . . " (KJV)
Hosea 3:4 " . . many days without king . . "

The near and far outpouring of the Holy Spirit—at Pentecost, and at the final Kingdom age.

Ezk.36:22, 27 " . . I will put my spirit within . . "

Ezk.37:1-27 "..can these bones live?..."
Joel 2:28 "..I will pour out my spirit.."

Two comings of the King of Kings are predicted—one to **Bethlehem** to die, and the other, still distant, to claim His **Kingdom**.

Micah 5:2 "..you..Bethlehem..from you shall come.."
Zech.12:10 "..whom they have pierced.." (cf. Matt.2:6)
Zech.14:4 "..on the Mount of Olives.."
Matt.1:18 "..betrothed to Joseph.."
Matt.2:1 "..born in Bethlehem.."

In the New Testament the coming of the kingdom was heralded by John the Baptist, and by Christ. The Jordan valley echoed with the news: "..with a cry of sensational and universal significance, the long-expected divine turning-point in history" was announced (NBD p.694). Demons were cast out—the power of Satan was broken. It was the main message of our Lord, and of the gospel preaching of the apostles.

Matt.3:2 "..the kingdom of heaven is at hand.."
Matt.4:17 "..Repent.." (It is to be a spiritual Kingdom)
Matt.5:3 et seq "..Blessed are the poor..the meek..the merciful..the pure..the peacemakers..for theirs is the Kingdom of heaven."
Matt.13:3 et seq... The seven **mysteries** of the Kingdom—the sower, the tares, the grain, the leaven etc.
Matt.17:1, 2, 5..The Transfiguration—A King!
Matt.21:5 "..thy King..upon an ass.." (KJV)
Matt.23:37 "..O Jerusalem, Jerusalem.."—He weeps.
Matt.27:37 "..THIS IS JESUS THE KING OF THE JEWS" (KJV) —nailed to the Cross.
John 19:14 "..'Here is your King!'.."
John 19:30 "..It is finished.."
Acts 1:3 "..speaking of the kingdom of God.."
Acts 1:6 "..restore the kingdom.."
Acts 1:11 "..will come in the same way.."
Acts 8:12 "..about the kingdom.."
Acts 14:22 "..must enter the kingdom.."
Acts 19:8 "..pleading about the kingdom.."
Acts 20:25 "..preaching the kingdom.."
Gal.5:17, 21 "..shall not inherit the kingdom.."
Col.1:13 "..transferred us to the kingdom.."
2 Thes. 1:5 "..worthy of the kingdom.."
James 2:5 "..heirs of the kingdom.."
Rev.19:16 "..KING OF KINGS.." in new Jerusalem! (KJV)

"Our Father who art in heaven
Hallowed be thy name
Thy kingdom come.." (Luke 11:2)

16: ASSURANCE—Confidence

What is meant by assurance? It "is the believer's full conviction that, through the work of Christ alone, received by faith, he is in possession of a salvation in which he will be eternally kept." This conviction should rest on faith in the unchanging God keeping His word, not on feelings which may change. Then as life proceeds he finds rest, knowing by experience that Christ dwelling within him can meet any emergency, and His blood cleanses any sin.

In the Old Testament assurance ".. is open to those who are righteous before God in any age."

Ps.37:1-7 ".. Trust.. Commit.. Be still.."
Prov.3:5, 6 ".. with all your heart.."
Is.32:17 ".. and assurance for ever.." (KJV)

There are two aspects of assurance. The immediate assurance of sonship is the heritage of every man on being born again, but the assurance of victory over sin is the promise for every truly surrendered Christian.

Rom.8:15, 16 ".. we are children of God.."
Rom.8:38, 39 ".. I am sure.."
1 Cor.10:13 ".. the way of escape.."
2 Tim.1:12 ".. he is able to guard.."
2 Tim.3:14, 15 ".. have firmly believed.."
2 Tim.4:8, 18 ".. Henceforth.. the crown.."
1 Peter 1:5 ".. are guarded.."
Jude 1 ".. kept for Jesus Christ.."

How is real assurance obtained? In the first place, by faith in God's word, also by confessing Christ with the lips before men. Then the assurance of victory rests on a pure conscience, honestly devoid of all barriers between ourselves and God or man. Where this is not so, the Holy Spirit convicts and assurance is shaken until the revealed thing is surrendered and forgiven by Christ. Beware of a false assurance which rests on success, self-effort, or the praise of men. (Matt.7:22, 23.)

Ps.17:8 ".. the apple of the eye.."
Ps.91:11 ".. his angels charge of you.."
Ps.103:12 ".. the east is from the west.."
Ps.121:3, 8 ".. not let your foot be moved.."
Is.26:3 ".. in perfect peace.."
Is.38:17 ".. behind thy back.."
Is.44:22 ".. like a cloud.."
Jer.31:34 ".. remember.. no more.."
John 5:24 ".. hears.. and believes.."
John 10:14 ".. I know my own.."
John 11:26 ".. shall never die.."
John 17:11 ".. Holy Father, keep them.."
Rom.8:28-34 ".. We know.."
Rom.10:9 ".. confess with your lips.."
Eph.1:13 ".. you.. were sealed.."
Phil.1:6 ".. I am sure.."

Col.2:2 " . . assured understanding . . "
Heb.7:25 " . . able for all time to save . . "
Heb.10:19, 22, 23 " . . we have confidence . . "
1 John 5:2, 18, 19, 20 " . . we know . . " (4 times)
Jude 24 " . . Now to him who is able to keep you . . "

17: TEMPTATION and TESTING

Temptation implies the means and enticements which the Devil employs to ensnare and allure mankind into sin, but sometimes the word temptation is used in the Bible in the sense of testing. The Devil tempts, but God tests. We must distinguish between the two.

"Temptation" is used in two senses in the Bible; (a) **Solicitation to evil**, and (b) **Testing under trial**.

    a. **Solicitation to evil**, which is not in itself sin, but may lead to it. From the beginning to the end of the Bible, Satan is revealed as the seducer of mankind, who beguiles and entices man into sin.

James 1:14 " . . but each person is tempted when he is lured and enticed by his own desire . . "
Gen.3:1-6, 13 " . . the serpent was more subtle . . "
Gen.12:13 " . . 'Say you are my sister' . . "
1 Chr.21:1 " . . Satan . . incited David . . "
Job 1:6 ff. " . . and Satan also came . . "
Matt.4:1 " . . Jesus . . tempted by the devil . . "
Matt.6:13 " . . 'lead us not into temptation' . . "
Matt.16:23 " . . 'Get behind me, Satan' . . "
Mark 4:15 " . . 'Satan immediately comes' . . "
Mark 14:38 " . . 'Watch and pray' . . "
Luke 22:31 " . . 'Satan demanded to have you' . . "
John 13:27 " . . Satan entered into him . . "
Acts 5:3 " . . 'Ananias, why has Satan' . . "
1 Cor.7:5 " . . lest Satan tempt you . . "
Heb.2:18 " . . he is able to help . . "
Heb.4:15 " . . in every respect . . "
James 1:14 " . . each person is tempted . . "
Rev.12:9 " . . the deceiver of the whole world . . "

    b. **Testing under trials**, which are allowed by God, can be strengthening. The godly are afflicted that they may be brought to self-knowledge, and to learn the secret of the "broken and contrite heart."

Gen.22:1 " . . God tested Abraham . . "
Job.1:12 " . . 'all that he has is in your power' . . " (to Satan)
Job 1:15-19 . . Testing by thieves, fire, whirlwind, he nearly dies, his children are killed and his wife wants him to die!
Job 3:11, 12 . . Job asks, " . . 'Why . . ? Why . . ? Why . . ?' . . "
Job 13:15 " . . Though he slay me, yet . . " (KJV)
Job 19:25 " . . 'my Redeemer lives' . . "
Job 23:10 " . . 'I shall come forth as gold' . . "
Job 42:10 " . . twice as much as . . before . . "
Acts 20:19 " . . 'and with tears' . . "
2 Cor.12:7 " . . thorn . . in the flesh . . to keep me from being too elated . . "
Gal.4:14 " . . though my condition was a trial to you . . "
1 Peter 1:6 " . . you may have to suffer . . "

Only those on the "Highway" know the secret of victory. God has provided a "way of escape". "Temptation becomes sin only when and as the suggestion of evil is accepted and yielded to." (NBD p.1251.) The moment this happens we must turn in repentance and confession to Christ for cleansing, and victory is restored (1 John 1:7-9).

1 Cor.10:13 ".. No temptation has overtaken you that is not common to man. God is faithful, and he will not let you be tempted beyond your strength, but with the temptation will also provide the way of escape, that you may be able to endure it.."

Eph.6:10-18 ".. stand against the wiles of the devil.."

1 Peter 5:8 ".. like a roaring lion.."

2 Peter 2:9 ".. the Lord knows how to rescue the godly from trial.."

18: SATAN—The Evil One

Who is Satan? The name comes from the Hebrew word *satan*, for "adversary", or "hater" (Greek *satanas*) but when the common noun is turned into a proper noun it becomes "Satan" (with a capital "S"), the Chief Adversary, the Arch-Enemy and the Deceiver of the whole world.

The Bible alone reveals his identity. Around his person centres the whole problem of evil, and the fall of man. He was once, in some mysterious way, an angel who held some high position in heaven. He sinned through pride and caused the fall of the whole human race. He is malignant, always hostile to God and to God's people, and is the personification of evil. He brings the "guilt complex" that haunts mankind.

Gen.3:1 " . . Now the serpent was more subtle . . "
1 Chr.21:1 " . . Satan . . incited David . . "
Job 1:6 " . . Satan also came . . "
Job 2:7 " . . and afflicted Job . . "
Is.14:12 " . . fallen from heaven, O Lucifer! . . " (KJV) (the beginning of sin in the universe).
Ezk.28:15 " . . till iniquity was found in you . . "
Ezk.28:17 " . . I cast you to the ground . . "
Zech.3:1 " . . Satan standing . . to accuse him . . "
Luke 10:18 " . . 'I saw Satan fall' . . "

Where is Satan now? He is called the "god of this world" (2 Cor.4:4,) also "the prince of the power of the air" (Eph.2:2). He has the power somehow to attract and beguile the whole world with worthless enticements, such as lust, greed, jealousy, fanatical ambition and worldly pleasures. The reward he gives of these things is emptiness of soul, sorrow, and death, just "chasing the wind". He has power to blind men's eyes, and Christians themselves are especially liable to more subtle attacks.

Rev.12:10 " . . the accuser . . " Greek *"diabolos"*.
Gen.3:4, 5 " . . 'You will not die' . . " He brings doubt.
John 8:44 " . . the father of lies . . " He brings unkind, unjust and untrue thoughts about others.
1 Cor.3:3, 4 " . . jealousy and strife among you . . " He knows how to bring divisions among Christian leaders, and over doctrine.
Matt.16:23 " . . 'Get behind me, Satan!' . . "
Matt.24:23, 24 " . . 'Lo, here is the Christ!' . . " He brings counterfeits.
Luke 22:31 " . . 'Simon . . Satan demanded to have you' . . "
John 8:44 " . . 'your father the devil' . . "
John 13:27 " . . Satan entered into him . . "
John 14:30 " . . 'the ruler of this world' . . "
Rom.5:12 " . . through one man . . spread to all men . . "
Rom.8:22 " . . whole creation has been groaning . . "
2 Cor.2:11 " . . not ignorant of his designs . . "
2 Cor.4:4 " . . has blinded the minds . . "
Eph.6:12 " . . not contending against flesh and blood . . "
Heb.2:14 " . . him who has the power of death . . "

1 Peter 5:8 " . . like a roaring lion . . "
1 John 2:16 " . . the lust of the flesh . . the pride of life . ."

Demons and demon-possession. The Bible speaks of "evil" and "unclean" spirits. They are evil and are the counterpart of the angels; mostly seen at the time of Christ's incarnation on earth, so there may be a resurgence in the last days. Demon-possession is a world-wide phenomenon, mostly among non-Christian peoples, signified in individuals by abnormal behaviour, changed facial expression, and voice.

Matt.12:24-29 . . Satan is compared with a foul heathen god,
" . . Be-elzebul . . prince of demons . . "
Matt.12:43 " . . When the unclean spirit . . "
Matt.25:41 " . . the devil and his angels . . "
Mark 5:9 " . . we are many . . " i.e. ubiquitous, worldwide.
Mark 5:8, 13 " . . 'Come out . . you unclean spirit!' . . "
Matt.8:16 . . Christ " . . cast out the spirits . . " et seq.
1 Tim.4:1–3 " . . doctrines of demons . . "

Acts 16:18 . . Exorcism in the name of Jesus Christ was practised by Paul. " . . 'I charge you in the name of Jesus Christ to come out of her' . . "

What is Satan's appointed end? The battle was fought and won by Christ in the wilderness when for forty days he faced Satan and returned "in the power of the Spirit", victorious over evil (Luke 4:14), to lead His band of disciples. But He began to make it plain that He would have to die on the Cross, and shed His blood as a lamb slain, before "the ruler of this world" (John 12:31) could be "cast out", and finally destroyed in "the lake of fire".

2 Cor.2:11 " . . Satan from gaining the advantage . . "
Heb.2:14 " . . he might destroy . . the devil . . "

There is now a way of escape from this relentless enemy Satan. We must be born again, and receive a new nature, through turning to Christ in repentance and faith, seeing Him crucified for us and Satan defeated. Satan got into the mob and they gave Him a crown of thorns, but it became a crown of glory. On the eve of the Cross He told the disciples to rejoice.

John 16:33 " . . be of good cheer . . "
James 4:7 " . . and he will flee . . "
Rom.16:20 " . . crush Satan under your feet . . "
1 Cor.15:26 " . . The last enemy . . destroyed . . "
1 Cor.10:13 " . . will also provide the way of escape . . "
2 Peter 1:4 " . . you may escape . . "
1 John 3:8 " . . who commits sin is of the devil . . "
1 John 4:4 " . . you . . have overcome . . "
Rev.20:2, 10 " . . he seized the dragon,
that ancient serpent,
who is the devil
and Satan,
and bound him . .
that he should deceive
the nations no more . .
and the devil was thrown
into the lake of fire . . "

19: SALVATION—The Cross

The death of our Lord Jesus Christ on the Cross is the focal point of history. The books of the Old Testament point to it, the Gospels describe it in detail, and the Epistles look back to it. The salvation of mankind is bound up with the Cross of Christ.

"They watched him there." (Matt.27:36 KJV.) The world still gazes at the Cross as onlookers. Christ bowed His head in obedience to His Father, and suffered for mankind on the Cross; and man must bow his head in repentance and thankfulness.

The word "salvation" is from the Latin *salvare* meaning "to save" or "to deliver from". Here it is taken in its theological sense of being saved from sin and eternal separation from God, and of being pardoned and received by Him.

In the Old Testament from earliest times the Cross was foreshadowed by the sacrifices which God had provided as a way of salvation for fallen man.

Gen.4:4 " . . for Abel and his offering . . " (cf. Heb.11.4) " . . Abel offered . . acceptable sacrifice . . "
Ex.12:11 " . . It is the Lord's passover . . "
Ex.30:10 " . . with the blood of the sin offering . . "
Lev.1:3 " . . without blemish . . "
Lev.17:11 " . . atonement for your souls . . "
Lev.23:5 " . . the Lord's passover . . " A yearly celebration.
Ps.22:1 " . . My God, my God, why hast thou forsaken me? . . "
—the cry from Christ on the Cross. This psalm contains a graphic description of the sufferings of crucifixion.
Ps.22:16 " . . pierced my hands and feet . . "
Ps.22:18 " . . they divide my garments . . cast lots . . "
Is.1:13 " . . no more vain offerings . . " the meaning of sacrifice forgotten.
Is.1:18 . . —but cleansing for sin provided.
Zech.12:10 " . . whom they have pierced . . "

In the New Testament the Gospels give the historical account of our Lord's death on the Cross, the place where Jesus Christ "died for our sins". (1 Cor.15:3.)

Matt.27:33 " . . a place called Golgotha . . "
Mark 15:24 " . . And they crucified him . . "
Luke 23:46 " . . he breathed his last . . "
Luke 24:25-27 . . Christ Himself interprets the Scriptures.
John 1:29 " . . 'Behold the Lamb of God' . . "
John 10:17 " . . 'I lay down my life' . . "
John 12:32 " . . 'when I am lifted up' . . "
John 17:4 " . . 'having accomplished the work' . . "
John 19:30 " . . he bowed his head . . "

The writers of the Epistles enlarged on the meaning of the Cross.

Rom.1:16 " . . the power of God for salvation . . "
1 Cor.1:23 " . . preach Christ crucified . . "

1 Cor.5:7 ".. Christ, our paschal lamb .."
1 Cor.6:20 ".. bought with a price .."
Gal.6:14 ".. glory .. in the cross .."
Eph.2:16 ".. reconcile .. through the cross .."
Phil.2:8 ".. humbled himself .. on a cross .."
Phil.3:18 ".. enemies of the cross .."
Col.1:20 ".. peace by the blood of his cross .."
Col.2:14 ".. nailing it to the cross .."
Heb.9:14 ".. how much more .."
Heb.10:1 ".. a shadow of the good things to come .."
1 Peter 1:19 ".. with the precious blood .."

What did our Lord mean by His words " .. be lifted up .. ? In the conversation recorded by John (ch. 3) Jesus reminded Nicodemus of how Moses had been told by God to make a serpent of brass, and to put it up on a pole. People who were dying of snake-bite could look at it and live.

NBC says (p.937): "The incident in the OT of Moses and the brazen serpent (Num.21:8, 9) is cited to illustrate the earthly work of the Son of man. The uplifting clearly refers to the cross..."

John 3:14a ".. as Moses lifted up the serpent .."
John 3.14b ".. so must the Son of man be lifted up .."
John 3:15 ".. may have eternal life .."
John 8:28 ".. When you have lifted up .. then you will know .."
Num.21:5 ".. the people spoke .. against Moses .."
Num.21:6 ".. fiery serpents .."
Num.21:7a ".. We have sinned .."
Num.21:7b ".. So Moses prayed for the people .."
Num.21:8, 9 ".. made a bronze serpent .. look .. and live .."
Num.21:17 ".. Israel sang this song .."

Devotional Note.

A picture from an old Bible. A full page etching shows Moses standing on a high rock, holding in his left hand a pole with the newly-forged brazen serpent, shining like gold in the setting sun. With his other hand he is trying to calm the frenzied people below. But in the picture there are four distinct groups at the foot of the rock.

(a) The *first* group are all *looking straight at Moses*, their great leader, thinking, "He has saved us before, he will save us again!" But they are falling down exhausted and dying one by one, with snakes all around them. They were trusting Moses instead of in God's command.

(b) The *second* group were *strong men with sticks and clubs*, pouring with perspiration, killing the snakes with all their might, but behind them and all around their ankles the snakes were biting, and they too were dying.

(c) The *third* group, *serious and devoted*, were going round tending to the sick and dying, too busy to look up at the healing pole, and dying like the others.

(d) The *last* group on the right *were all standing calmly looking straight at the brazen serpent* held out by Moses and were singing praises to God and calling to the others.

The message of this old etching is summed up in the words of the hymn of A.M.Hull:

> There is life for a look at the crucified One,
> There is life at this moment for thee;
> Then look, sinner, look unto Him, and be saved,
> Unto Him Who was nailed to the tree.

20: SALVATION—The New Birth

The new birth is a necessity for salvation. It is the change of heart and life that a man experiences when he becomes a true Christian. But as a child cannot beget itself no more can a carnal man regenerate himself. The new birth is the operation of the Holy Spirit in the heart and life of a man who accepts Christ. It is an event in life; it is man's second birthday. It takes place within him when he repents of his sin and yields his life to Christ, and believes in Him as Saviour.

The natural man is blind to the things of God. Sin must be cleansed and the evil nature rendered powerless.

Ps.51:5 " . . Behold, I was brought forth in iniquity . . "
Jer.17:9 " . . The heart is deceitful . . "
Mark 7:21 " . . out of the heart of man come evil thoughts,
   fornication, theft, murder . . "
Rom.6:6 " . . that the sinful body might be destroyed . . "
1 Cor.2:14 " . . The unspiritual man . . is not able to understand . . "
Eph.2:3 " . . by nature children of wrath . . "

The decision is a step taken deliberately and carefully in faith. After repenting, and trusting in the blood of Jesus to cleanse from sin, the new birth mysteriously follows. This sonship is given to us once and for all. A child of God can unhappily backslide, but still remains a child of God. After backsliding he must come back in humble penitence, but this does not mean "being born again" a second or third time.

Matt.18:3 " . . unless you turn . . "
John 1:12 " . . children of God . . "
John 3:15 " . . whoever believes in him . . "
John 5:24 " . . passed from death to life . . "
Acts 3:19 " . . Repent therefore, and turn again . . "
Acts 16:30 " . . what must I do to be saved? . . "

It is not a self-reformation but a creative act of the Holy Spirit brought about by the hearing of the Word. Man has no power to work the change. It is not something that happens automatically by Baptism.

John 3:3 " . . unless one is born anew . . "
Rom.8:16 " . . the Spirit himself bearing witness . . "
2 Cor.5:17 " . . in Christ, he is a new creation . . "
Gal.6:15 " . . a new creation . . "
Titus 3:5 " . . not . . by us in righteousness . . regeneration . . in
   the Holy Spirit . . "

The new life must grow after the new birth, and the believer will witness to the change. He has become a partaker of the Divine Nature and Life of Christ Himself, because all are "led by the Spirit" and become "sons of God . . and fellow heirs with Christ."

John 5:6 " . . 'Do you want to be healed?' . . "
John 5:15 " . . The man . . told the Jews that it was Jesus who
   had healed him . . "

Rom.6:23 ".. the free gift .. eternal life .. "
Rom.8:14 ".. led by the Spirit .. "
Rom.8:17 ".. children .. heirs with Christ .. "
Eph.2:1-5 ".. you he made alive .. "
Eph.2:10 ".. created .. for good works .. "
Col.3:1 ".. raised with Christ .. "
Col.3:10 ".. have put on the new nature .. being renewed .. "
Titus 2:11, 12 ".. salvation .. to live .. godly lives .. "
1 Peter 1:3 ".. born anew to a living hope .. "
1 Peter 1:23 ".. You have been born anew .. "
1 John 5:11 ".. God gave us eternal life .. in His Son .. "

When our Lord said to Nicodemus—"Except a man be born again he cannot *see* the kingdom of God." (John 3:3 KJV) what did He mean by this?

NBC explains this—".. only those who take the step of faith to enter can be said .. to 'see' the Kingdom. 'Seeing' in this sense may be understood as experiencing" (p.936).

Matt.18:3 ".. become like children .. "
John 3:8 ".. born of the Spirit .. "
John 5:24 ".. has passed from death to life .. "

Devotional Note.

John Bunyan, in his immortal allegory of Christian losing his burden at the Cross, makes this *"seeing"* more clear.

Now I saw in my dream that the highway up which Christian was to go, was fenced on either side with a wall that was called Salvation. Up that way, therefore did burdened Christian run. He ran thus till he came to a place somewhat ascending; and upon that place stood a Cross, and a little below, in the bottom a sepulchre. So I saw in my dream that just as Christian came up with the Cross, his burden loosed from off his shoulders, and fell from off his back, and began to tumble, and so continued to do till it came to the mouth of the sepulchre, where it fell in and I saw it no more.

Then was Christian glad and lightsome, and said with a merry heart, "He hath given me rest by His sorrow, and life by His death."

Then he stood still awhile to look and wonder; for it was very surprising to him that the sight of the Cross should thus ease him of his burden. He looked again, even till the springs that were in his head sent the water down his cheeks...

Then Christian gave three leaps for joy, and went on singing.

21: PRAYER—Communication with God

Prayer is communion between man and his Maker. It is an attitude of mind rather than an attitude of body, and it is a result of faith, rather than a repetition of wants. It is fallen man's way of "tuning in" to God, and in some mysterious way it is God's means of liberating His power on earth. It is a universal urge of man, who is made in the image of God.

In the Old Testament men prayed, appealing to God as merciful and gracious, and also with the eyes of faith, we believe, seeing their redemption which lay behind all the sacrifices.

Gen.18:23, 32 " . . 'Wilt thou . . destroy the righteous?' . . "
Gen.32:9–11 " . . 'O God of my father Abraham' . . "
Ex.32:11–13 " . . But Moses besought the Lord . . "
Ex.33:12–16 " . . Moses said . . 'show me now thy way' . . "
Num.10:35 " . . Moses said, 'Arise, O Lord' . . "
Num.14:17–19 " . . And now, I pray thee . . "
Judges 16:28 " . . Samson called to the Lord . . "
1 Sam.1:11 " . . she vowed a vow . . "
1 Kings 8:22, 23 " . . Solomon stood before the altar . . "
Neh.1:6 " . . 'I now pray before thee . . confessing the sins' . . "
Ps.57:9 " . . I will give thanks . . "
Jonah 2:1 " . . Then Jonah prayed . . "
Hab.3:2 " . . thy work . . in the midst of the years renew it . . "

In the New Testament after Christ came, a new intimacy was revealed. He taught His disciples to pray on a new basis, that of relationship. By the new birth we are made children, and can speak to God as our Father. Christ revealed this new relationship in person as He lived His life amongst men. He taught them to lift up their eyes and hearts to God at all hours of the day and night, in any place, or in any circumstances, as children speak to their father. In this new intimacy there is no place for "vain repetitions", or praying "to be seen of men", for He is the Father who sees in secret and reads the heart.

Matt.6:9 " . . 'Pray then like this' . . "
Matt.11:25, 26 " . . 'I thank thee, Father' . . "
Matt.26:41 " . . 'Watch and pray' . . "
Mark 1:35 " . . a great while before day . . "
Luke 11:1 " . . 'Lord, teach is to pray' . . "
Luke 15:18 " . . 'Father, I have sinned' . . "
John 14:13 " . . 'Whatever you ask' . . "
John 17:1 " . . Jesus . . lifted up his eyes . . " The most wonderful prayer ever prayed.
Matt.26:39 " . . 'not as I will, but as thou wilt' . . " The most wonderful submission; in Gethsemane.
Luke 23:34 " . . 'Father, forgive them; for they know not what they do' . . " The most wonderful forgiveness from the; Cross.

After Pentecost the new relationship becomes a deeper and a fuller experience still. The children of God grow to the full manhood of grown-up sons and daughters. Thus prayer takes place "in the Heavenlies" with Christ

Jesus. But it must be prayer in the Spirit, submitting our desires to Him and seeking His guidance as to what we pray for. We pray sometimes under a deep sense of urgency, with a feeling of a real burden on our hearts, and this may well be because the Holy Spirit is impelling us unconsciously within, and speaking through us in our prayers. This is the prayer that removes mountains. This is where we ask and receive.

Luke 9:28, 29 " . . as he was praying . . his countenance was altered . . "
Luke 22:44 " . . being in an agony . . "
Acts 4:31 " . . the place . . was shaken . . "
Acts 9:5, 11 " . . 'Who art thou, Lord?' . . " (KJV)
Acts 10:9 " . .Peter . . on the housetop to pray . . "
Acts 12:5, 7, 11, 12 " . . Peter . . in prison . . the chains fell off . . "
Acts 16:13 " . . to the riverside . . a place of prayer . . "
Acts 21:5 " . . on the beach we prayed . . "
Rom.8:26, 27 " . . with sighs too deep for words . . "
Eph.1:3 " . . in the heavenly places . . "
Eph.6:18 " . . prayer and supplication . . "
Col.4:3 " . . open to us a door . . "
1 Thess.3:10 " . . night and day . . "
1 Tim.2:8 " . . lifting holy hands . . "
James 5:16 " . . The effectual fervent prayer . . " (KJV)
Jude 20 " . . pray in the Holy Spirit . . "

Prayer is conditional.
Ps.66:18 " . . iniquity in my heart . . "
Mark 11:25 " . . anything against any one . . "

Quiet times for meditation, solitude, private devotion and contemplation are essential, and "to pray without words" (Matt.6:8).

Dan.6:10 " . . upon his knees three times a day . . "
Dan.9:3-5 " . . I turned my face . . with fasting . . "
Mark 1:35 " . . a great while before day . . "
1 Cor.14:15 " . . with the spirit and . . with the mind . . "

Victorious praying. Prayer in fellowship, or house-groups, or in ones or twos, when all are deeply of "one accord" at the Cross, and are completely united in the love of and for Christ. This is the place of Revival.

Acts. 1:14 " . . All these with one accord devoted themselves to prayer . . "
Matt.18:20 " . . 'there am I in the midst of them' . . "
Rom.8:26 The Spirit Himself " . . maketh intercession for us with groanings which cannot be uttered . . " (KJV)

The following simple mnemonic, from the folding of the hands in prayer, may help some people in organising their times of prayer:

(a) The *thumb*—turning over the pages of the Bible, *Bible Study* daily.
(b) The *first finger*—be quiet and listen to the *Holy Spirit* speaking through the Word.
(c) The *middle finger*—the most important one: *Prayer*.
(d) The *ring finger*—your home, your *plans*, for each day.
(e) The *little finger*—*write* it down—it is so easy to forget!
Two hands—*morning* and *evening*.

22: COMPROMISE—Separation from the world

What does separation mean? It does *not* necessarily mean the life of an ascetic, or to shut oneself up in a monastery. But spiritually, for the true Christian it means the power to live "in the world, but not of the world", i.e. the desire for worldly things and pleasures is replaced and overcome by the new nature of Christ, which fills the heart. Compromise with evil in any form hinders blessing for a Christian. Paul says: "Be ye not unequally yoked together with unbelievers . . "

2 Cor.6:14–17 " . . what fellowship . . with darkness ? . . "
1 John 2:15–17 " . . Do not love the world . . "
Rev.18:4, 5 " . . 'Come out of her, my people' . . "

Separation from the world is well illustrated by the story of the Israelites coming out of Egypt—Pharaoh represents the Adversary—on their trying to leave Egypt Pharaoh offered his compromises.

(a) *The first compromise:* "Sacrifice to your God, *in* the land", i.e. "Be a Christian where you are"—"Do your best"—"Why be born again?"—"You need not leave the land of Egypt."

Ex.2:10, 11 . . Moses " . . went out to his people . . "
Ex.6:6 " . . 'I will bring you out' . . "
Ex.7:14 . . (Pharaoh) " . . 'refuses to let the people go' . . "
Ex.8:25 " . . 'Go, sacrifice to your God within the land' . . "

(b) *The second compromise:* "Only you shall not go very far away", i.e. "Be a Christian but don't be a narrow one"—"Don't go too far"—"Don't be like so-and-so."

Ex.8:28 " . . Pharaoh said, 'I will let you go . . only you shall not go very far away' . . "
Eph.5:11 . . Paul said, " . .Take no part in the unfruitful works of darkness . . "

(c) *The third compromise:* "Go now, ye that are men . . ", i.e. "Be a Christian yourself, but it doesn't matter about your home, and your married life", i.e. your thoughts and sex-life may still be in Egypt.

Ex.10:11 " . . 'Go, the men among you' . . "

(d) *The fourth compromise:* "Go ye . . only let your flocks and herds be stayed", i.e. "Be a Christian, but it doesn't matter what your business relationships are"; you may be known as a keen Christian family, but your business affairs and your money are still in Egypt.

Ex.10:24 . . Pharaoh said, " . . 'let your flocks and your herds remain behind' . . "
1 Sam.15:9 " . . But Saul and the people spared Agag . . the best of the sheep . . "
1 Sam.15:13, 14 " . . 'I have performed the commandment of the Lord'. Samuel said 'What then is this bleating' . . "
1 Sam.15:22, 23 " . . 'rebellion . . and stubbornness . . as iniquity and idolatry' . . "

Moses was adamant . . "Not a hoof shall be left behind," and he adds to Pharaoh, "I will not see your face again." From then he prepares to leave the land. Cf. Paul's words: "Come out from among them, and be ye separate."

Ex.10:26 " . . 'not a hoof shall be left behind' . . "
Ex.10:29 " . . 'I will not see your face again' . . "
So for the Christian there must be no compromise with sin. Cf. further references from Genesis to Revelation:
Gen.12:1 " . . the Lord said to Abram, 'Go . . to the land that I will show you' . . "
Gen.13:12 " . . Lot . . moved his tent as far as Sodom . . "
Ex.33:16 " . . 'we are distinct' . . "
Lev.20:24 " . . 'the Lord your God . . separated you' . . "
Deut.22:10 " . . 'not plow with an ox and an ass together' . . "
Ezra 6:21 " . . from the pollutions of the peoples . . "
Neh.9:2 " . . separated themselves . . and confessed their sins . . "
John 15:18, 19 . . Christ's words—" . . 'you are not of the world' . . "
John 17:6, 14-17 . . Christ's words—" . . 'out of the world' . . "
Rom.12:2 . . Paul said—" . . Do not be conformed to this world . ."
1 Cor.5:2, 6, 7, 13 " . . Cleanse out the old leaven . . "—(sexual immorality).
1 Cor.10:20, 21 " . . not . . partners with demons . . "— i.e. paganism.
2 Thess.3:6, 14 " . . keep away from . . "
1 Tim.6:6 " . . There is a great gain in godliness with contentment . . "
2 Tim.2:19-26 " . . 'depart from iniquity' . . "
Heb.11:24, 25 " . . Moses . . refused . . fleeting pleasures of sin . . "
Heb.13:13 " . . without the camp, bearing his reproach . . " (KJV)
Rev.21:27 " . . nothing unclean shall enter it . . "

23: THE WILDERNESS LIFE—The "Up and Down" Life

The story of the Israelites coming out of the bondage of Egypt, and passing through the wilderness to the Promised Land is full of deep meaning for all Christians. There were landmarks of experience.

I Cor.10:11 " . . all these things happened . . for ensamples: and for our admonition . . " (KJV)

Instructions on setting out. Remember the day you decided. There will be "the pillar of cloud" by day, and "the pillar of fire" by night, to guide you. "be firm and brave, never be daunted or dismayed for . . your God is with you wherever you go." Josh.1:9 (Moffatt's translation).

Ex.13:3, 17 " . . Remember this day, in which you came out from Egypt . . "
Ex.13:18 " . . God led the people round by the way of the wilderness . . "
Ex.13:20–22 " . . by day in a pillar of cloud . . and by night in a pillar of fire . . "

Experience 1. Fear. The Egyptians behind—the Red Sea in front—they looked fools! But God said: "stand still", and later they saw the bodies of their enemies dead upon the seashore. What are these fears that haunt the Christian? They are, fear of ridicule, failure, disease, poverty and the like.

Ex.14:3, 10, 11, 12 " . . 'it would have been better for us to serve the Egyptians than to die in the wilderness' . . "
Ex.14:14, 19 " . . the angel of God . . moved and went behind them . . "
Ex.14:30 " . . the Egyptians dead upon the seashore . . "
cf. Is.41:10 " . . fear not, for I am with you . . "
Is.58:8 " . . the glory of the Lord shall be your rear-guard . . "

Experience 2. Thirst. The water was bitter, e.g. our work, or our companions may be uncongenial—*but* the tree made it sweet, i.e. Christ alone can sweeten all life's hardships (cf. the Cross).

Ex.15:22 " . . and found no water . . "
Ex.15:23 " . . the water . . was bitter . . "
Ex.15:25 " . . the Lord showed him a tree . . the water became sweet . . "
Ex.15:27 " . . Elim . . twelve springs of water . . they encamped there . . "
Rom.5:3 " . . we rejoice in our sufferings . . "

Experience 3. Complaining. The food ran short—they grumbled—but Moses pointed out that they were complaining against God, the One Who had saved them. Moses says: " . . your murmurings are not against us, but against the Lord." Grumbling is the sympton of a starved soul, i.e. the "Quiet Time" crowded out, Bible study neglected, prayer curtailed.

Ex.16:2 " . . the whole congregation . . murmured . . "

Ex.16:8, 12 " . . in the morning bread to the full . . "
Phil.2:14 " . . Do all things without grumbling or questioning . . "

Experience 4. Hunger. They were hungry—the sign of the starved soul (cf. experience 3), but God gave them manna, the "bread from heaven". The Word of God is the Bread of Life, to be taken fresh every day.

Ex.16:3 " . . 'Would that we had died . . in . . Egypt' . . "
Ex.16:4 " . . 'gather . . every day' , , "
Ex.16:21 " . . Morning by morning they gathered it . . "
John 6:33–35 " . . Jesus said . . 'I am the bread of life' . . "
John 6:41, 49, 51 " . . 'I am the bread which came down from heaven' . . "

Experience 5. Doubt and Despair. They said: "Is the Lord with us or not?" i.e. "Am I really converted after all?" "I cannot go further." "I do not like the way." "I" instead of "Him". Then God sent Moses to pray on the mountain, and allowed the Amalakites to test and try them. We fight "the flesh", but Christ, the Intercessor, wins the victory. Doubts bring internal conflict, but Moses pleaded "till the going down of the sun". Christ "ever liveth to make intercession for us."

Ex.17:7 " . . 'Is the Lord among us, or not?' . . "
Ex.17:8, 9 " . . then came Amalek and fought . . "
Ex.17:11 " . . whenever Moses held up his hand . . "
Ex.17:15 " . . And Moses built an altar . . "
Rom.7:24, 25 " . . who will deliver me . . Jesus Christ . . "
Rom.8:26–28 " . . the Spirit helps us in our weakness . . "
Gal.5:17 " . . For the desires of the flesh are against the Spirit . . "

Experience 6. Idol Worship. Moses and the pillar of cloud were temporarily lost sight of; faith grew dim and the people demanded something that they could see on which to centre their worship. It appears that Aaron at least intended the calf to represent Jehovah. This is the danger of mass media, ideologies, hero worship and "aids to worship." Sensuality had come in, " . . for Aaron had made them naked unto their shame . . " Ex.32:25. There was no turning to God, so all this degenerated into worldliness and sensuality. But Moses pleads, with a broken heart, one of the most wonderful prayers of the Bible—so the Spirit ever pleads for us still, "with groanings that cannot be uttered."

Ex.32:1–8 " . . 'turned aside quickly out of the way' . . "
Ex.32:9 " . . it is a stiff-necked people' . . "
Ex.32:22 . . Aaron blamed the people, not himself.
Ex.32:32 . . Moses pleads, " . . 'if not, blot me, I pray thee, out of thy book' . . ", and breaks down.

As a child led by the hand, so God brings this fractious and rebellious people to the border of the Promised Land.

cf. Matt.4:1 . . Christ went into this wilderness for forty days
& Heb.4:15 to be tempted. " . . yet without sinning . . "

24: THE VICTORIOUS LIFE—"Not I but Christ"

On the threshold of the Promised Land. The children of Israel, in spite of their many mistakes, had come to the borders of their Promised Land. They could see the green hills and the mountains away to the west across the Jordan Valley. It was Passover time in the spring. As at first after leaving Egypt they receive their orders from God Himself, "Go!", "Enter in."

Victory was promised. The twelve spies went in to spy out the land, and even tasted of the very fruit of the land, and came back with their report, but the people remained obstinate. The giants of the land loomed large, and they were afraid. These giants typify our free wills which can sway us. God will not force us against our wills.

Joshua 1:2 " . . 'arise, go over this Jordan' . . "

In Christian experience what can "the giants" represent ? Many Christians never enter into rest, true peace, and victory (i.e. resting in the finished work of Christ). Many Christian homes are ruined by these giants. Many have even ceased to believe that there *is* a promised land! All these giants centre in "self".

1. **The Giant "I"—"Self".** This is mistrust of God. If we heed it our faith grows dim and we begin to fear. We say to God, "I'm too weak"—"I can't forgive so-and-so"—"So-and-so is more gifted than I am, or better-off, or better-looking, or more clever." Or we may say, "I can't do this"—"I'm not made that way"—"I don't believe it's possible for me". It is "I" instead of "HIM". This has been called the Idolatry of believers.

    The self must be crucified with Christ, and when it is surrendered and repented of, the giant "Unbelief" dies. The Cross is the "I" crossed out.

    Ex.32:9 " . . a stiff-necked people . . "
    Num.13:32, 33 " . . an evil report . . giants . . we were . . as grasshoppers . . " (KJV)
    Num.14:8, 9 . . Joshua pleaded " . . 'do not rebel against the Lord' . . " They had faith to sprinkle the blood of atonement in Egypt, but no faith now to enter in.
    Jer.1:7-9 " . . 'Do not say "I am only a youth" ' . . "
    Amos 7:14, 15 " . . 'I am no prophet' . . the Lord said . . 'Go, prophesy' . . "
    Mark 6:5, 6 " . . he could do no mighty work . . and he marvelled because of their unbelief . . "
    Heb.3:12 " . . Take care, brethren, lest there be in any of you an evil, unbelieving heart . . "

2. **The Giant "Apathy" or "Drift".** We allow the rush of modern life to carry us with it. We say "I've no time for these things"—"I'm too busy"—"I'll wait till I'm older"—"Till I've finished my exams"—"Till I retire"! We allow ourselves to be swamped by our work. The giant "procrastination" steals away the blessing. Our birthright of real life is bartered for the passing comfort of a "mess of pottage" (cf. Jacob and Esau).

    Gen.25:32 " . . 'of what use is a birthright to me' . . "
    Matt.13:22 " . . 'the cares of the world . . choke the word' . . "
    Heb.2:1 " . . lest we drift away . . "

3. The Giant "Self-Righteousness". This is the unwillingness, or apparent inability, of so many Christians to realise their need. Let us beware of "blind spots" and unforgiveness.

> Luke 18:11 " . . 'The Pharisee . . prayed thus with himself' . . "
> Rev.3:17 " . . 'not knowing that you are wretched, pitiable, poor, blind' . . "

4. The Giant "Self-Deception". This is insincerity and dishonesty in all its various forms amongst Christians such as "bluff", "sham heartiness", "pose", "wearing a mask", "dodging responsibility"—and all hypocrisy. There can be no real fellowship if we are afraid of being transparent and of walking "in the light, as he is in the light" (1 John 1:7). Much insincerity is the result of fear in some form. Under this heading comes "exaggeration", and even "lies".

> Heb.4:12, 13 " . . the word of God is living . . discerning the thoughts and intentions of the heart . . "

5. The Giant "Self-Indulgence". It is easy, as we have free wills, to allow self-indulgence to begin in a small way, especially in such things as love of ease, food, drink, and sensual excitements. Impurity and maladjustment in sexual things all too often follow and lead many deep into the wilderness.

> Mark 7:20–23 " . . 'out of the heart . . come evil thoughts' . . "
> 1 Cor.9:24–27 " . . I keep under my body . . " (KJV)
> 1 Cor.10:6, 13 " . . way of escape . . "

6. The Giant "Self-Centredness". There may be things that we are determined not to yield to Christ—long standing sins that have become part of our very selves such as pride of race, or degrees, love of praise or money, desire to be first, envy, indifference to the needs and rights of others, self-glorification, disparagement of others. The self-centred life mars the "rest" of so many Christians. If we have "blind spots" towards these things, a faithful friend may help us to see ourselves as we really are in God's sight, so that we can bring the sins to Christ for victory. This giant may lead Christians to become vindictive and cruel when they are crossed.

> Rom.12:3, 10 " . . outdo one another in showing honour . . "
> Gal.5:26 " . . no envy of one another . . "
> 1 Tim.6:10 " . . love of money is the root of all evils . . "

7. The Giant "Self-Pity". All unsurrendered pent-up sorrow, self-pity and whining, "the martyr spirit", in all their various forms, are wrong, and if nursed and dwelt upon will grow and obscure the vision of victory; negativeness is a reflection of inner defeat. These lead on often to Giant Despair. Tiredness is often due to indiscipline. Grousing and complaining (even about the weather) become a habit, and are sins. Moses called the murmuring Israelites and said: "your murmurings are not against us but against the Lord." Are you blaming God for something? Augustine prayed: "Lord save me from self-vindication." Are you saying that God has "let you down over something?" Paul and the early Christians rejoiced in suffering in Christ's cause.

> Acts 5:41 " . . rejoicing . . to suffer . . for the name . . "
> Rom.5:4 " . . endurance produces character . . "
> 2 Cor.12:10 " . . I am content with weaknesses . . "

Phil.4:12, 13 " . . to be abased . . to abound . . "
2·Cor11:27 " . . through many a sleepless night . . "

8. The Giant "Self-Consciousness". This robs many of peace in Christ and joy in witness. It causes shyness, loneliness and strain, which sometimes are forms of pride, and it may lead to inability to work with others. Fellowship is God's plan for Christians, and is the very hall-mark of live Christianity and revival.

Ex.4:10 " . . 'I am not eloquent' . . "
Judges 6:15 " . . 'I am the least' . . "
Jer.1:8 " . . 'Be not afraid of them' . . "
Luke 10:1 " . . sent them . . two by two . . "
Acts 1:14 " . . All . . with one accord . . "

9. The Giant "Self-Defence". By this we mean "excusing oneself for one's failures", especially by running down and decrying others. We say, for example, "I've no use for this holiness teaching". We hit back, abuse and criticise—the sin of "sour grapes", and "pointing the finger".

Luke 11:15 " . . 'by . . the prince of demons' . . "
Luke 23:2 " . . they began to accuse him . . "
Acts 2:13 " . . others mocking said . . 'filled with new wine' . . "
Acts 26:24 " . . 'you are mad' . . "

The Forty Years Wandering. The doubt of ten of the twelve chosen leaders, about the possibility of entering in, quickly spread to the mass of the people who were waiting for their report. The more they talked about it and compared their own strength with that of the enemy, the more their doubt grew, till the whole multitude turned their backs on the land. They grew angry and blamed and cursed God. This resulted in the punishment of forty years of wandering.

This story seems to teach us the solemn lesson that we may ourselves fail to enter into the Christian's promised land, which is the fullness of the Spirit. This experience is promised to all; it is the gift of Pentecost. Some form of passing through the wilderness is an almost invariable experience. "The wilderness was part of the necessary discipline of the redeemed people, but *not* the years of wandering."

Num.14:1–3 " . . the people wept that night . . "
Num.14:22, 23, 33 . . All the giants haunted them and filled them
with rebellion and anger. They even wanted to stone Joshua
and Caleb, till the Lord said " . . 'you . . shall wander in the
wilderness forty years' . . " (KJV)
1 Cor.10:1–11 " . . written down for our instruction . . "
Heb.3:8, 12 " . . 'do not harden your hearts' . . an evil,
unbelieving heart . . "

The Final Commands. After the forty years of wandering were ended, they were again told to enter in thus: "Do not be afraid"—"Go in and possess the land." God promised rest in place of wandering, rest in place of struggling, rest in the finished work of Christ on the cross.

Deut.1:6, 8 " . . 'You have stayed long enough at this mountain' . . "
Deut.6:5 " . . 'love the Lord . . with all your heart' . . "

Deut.30:19 " . . 'therefore choose life' . . "
Joshua 1:2 " . . 'now therefore arise, go over this Jordan' . . "
Cf. Paul's experience:
Rom.7:24, 25 " . . who will deliver me ? . . Thanks be to God through Jesus Christ our Lord . . "

The Entry into the Promised Land. The passing over the Jordan was a miracle. The order was "Sanctify yourselves: for tomorrow the Lord will do wonders among you." In the early hours of the morning the power of God came down as the twelve priests carrying the ark went ahead down into the Jordan. Up river the flood was stopped and the priests were followed by the whole disiplined, desert people, every man, woman and child witnessing the redemptive power of God, symbolised in the Ark of the Covenant, holding back the waters while the priests stood firm in the midst of Jordan, till " . . all . . were passed clean over . . "

They formed up on the other side, with Joshua at their head. Then God intervened in the likeness of a man with a drawn sword, causing Joshua to fall down in worship. The Captain of the host of the Lord had come in person to lead them into the land.

Joshua 3:5 " . . 'Sanctify yourselves' . . "
Joshua 5:13–15 " . . 'as commander of the army of the Lord I have now come' . . "

The secret of the victorious life was demonstrated before all the people, and can be summed up in Paul's words to the Galatians:

Gal.2:20 " . . Not I, but Christ . . " (KJV)
A prayer: Lord, bend that proud and stiff-necked "I",
             Help me to bow the neck and die,
             Beholding Him on Calvary,
             Who bowed His head for me.

25: THE HOLY SPIRIT—The Third Person of the Trinity

The Holy Spirit is the third Person of the Trinity. He shares in the creation. He is likened to the wind, fire, and water. He inspires men to build, to plant, to make beautiful things; to speak, to preach, to laugh and to sing, and to make music. He gives courage, bravery, leadership and fearless testimony. He gives visions, dreams and divine revelation. He gives people respect, caring, courtesy and love. He gives true fear of God, and understanding of the blood of Christ as God's remedy for sin, and can unveil the future and make men seers and prophets. He helps men to pray, and to intercede with God. He helps men to bow their stubborn wills, to repent, to humble themselves, to yield and so to be set free. And lastly He wakens, He revives, He gives the burning heart, and He lights up the faces of men and women to be truly Christlike.

In the Old Testament the Holy Spirit came upon men for special tasks, to lead God's people through the wilderness to the Promised Land, to write the sacred Scriptures, to inspire the deep inner meaning of the Tabernacle, and to light up the Holy of Holies and the Mercy-Seat, where a holy God met sinful men on the basis of atoning sacrifice.

Then, after repeated warnings about apostasy, through the prophets, He points to the coming Messiah. The personality of the Holy Spirit appears from the attributes ascribed to Him.

Gen.1:2 " . . the Spirit of God was moving over the face of the waters . . "

Ex.28:3 " . . make Aaron's garments . . "

Ex.31:3 . . For the building of the Tabernacle.

Num.11:26–29 . . A foretaste of Pentecost, prophesying.

Num.27:18 " . . Joshua . . in whom is the spirit . . "

Judges 3:10 " . . Othniel . . the Spirit of the Lord came upon him . . "

Judges 6:34 " . . the Spirit of the Lord took possession of Gideon . . "

2 Sam.23:1, 2 " . . David . . the sweet psalmist . . "

2 Chron.24:20, 21 . . Zechariah stoned calling people to repent. The spirit of the martyrs.

Is.32:15 " . . Until the spirit is poured upon us . . "

Is.44:3 " . . floods upon the dry ground . . " (KJV)

Is.61:1 " . . to bring good tidings . . "

Joel 2:28, 29 " . . I will pour out . . on all flesh . . "

Zech.4:6 " . . Not by might . . but by my Spirit . . "

Zech.12:10 " . . a spirit of compassion and supplication . . "

In the New Testament the Holy Spirit still came upon individuals. First upon Mary, for the miraculous birth of the Messiah, and upon Zacharias and John the Baptist from his birth, and for opening the eyes of Simeon. Then John announced Jesus, and " . . heaven was opened, and the Holy Ghost descended . . like a dove . . "

The Holy Spirit watched over the battle, fought out in the wilderness, for the redemption of the world, by the Lord Jesus.

Matt.1:18 " .. she was found to be with child of the Holy Spirit .. "
Matt.3:11 " .. baptize you with the Holy Spirit .. "
Matt.10:20 " .. the Spirit of your Father .. through you .. "
Luke 1:15 .. John the Baptist " .. filled with the Holy Spirit .."
Luke 1:67 " .. Zachariah was filled with the Holy Spirit .. "
Luke 2:25-27 " .. Simeon .. inspired by the Spirit, he came into the temple .. "
Luke 3:22 " .. descended .. as a dove .. "
Luke 4:1 " .. Jesus .. led by the Spirit .. in the wilderness .. "
John 3:5 " .. unless one is born .. of the Spirit .. "
John 7:37 " .. if any one thirst .. "
John 7:39 " .. about the Spirit .. had not been given .. "
John 14:16, 17 " .. another Comforter .. the Spirit of truth .. " (KJV)
John 16:7, 8 " .. it is to your advantage that I go away .. "
John 20:22 " .. he breathed on them .. Receive the Holy Spirit .. "

On the Day of Pentecost—and after. The disciples, after being abject failures, learned the secret of receiving the Holy Spirit. They had to be beggars, repentant and united, with their hands empty, and stretched out in supplication, and to wait for the promise. With the sound of a rushing wind and tongues of fire, they were all filled with the Holy Spirit. The love of God was poured out upon those in the upper room, and then to the crowd that collected outside, and then went on to change the world.

Acts 1:4, 8 " .. wait for the promise .. "
Acts 1:14 " .. in prayer and supplication .. " (KJV)
Acts 2:1-7 " .. Pentecost .. all filled with the Holy Spirit .. "
Acts 2:18, 38 " .. Repent .. and you shall receive .. "
Acts 4:8,31 .. Peter, a second filling!
Acts 7:55 .. Stephen, the first martyr.
Acts.8:18-22 " .. your silver perish with you .. " Simon the Sorcerer.
Acts 10:44, 45 " .. the Holy Spirit fell .. even on the Gentiles .."
Acts 13:2, 4 " .. set apart for me Barnabas and Saul .. "

The doctrine of the Holy Spirit is further expounded by Paul and other writers of the Epistles.

Our bodies become the temples of the Holy Spirit.

The fruit, with love in all its aspects, of the Spirit will be seen in our lives, but there are diversities of gifts—wisdom—healing—tongues—all given for one purpose—that of preaching "Christ and Him crucified."

Rom.5:5 " .. God's love .. poured into our hearts .. "
Rom.8:2 .. Paul's testimony, " .. the Spirit of life in Christ Jesus .. "
Rom.14:17 " .. joy in the Holy Spirit .. "
1 Cor.2:4 " .. and power .. "
1 Cor.3:16 " .. you are God's temple .. "
2 Cor.13:14 " .. the fellowship of the Holy Spirit .. "
Gal.5:16 " .. walk by the Spirit .. "
Eph.4:30 " .. do not grieve the Holy Spirit .. "
Eph.6:17 " .. take .. the sword of the Spirit .. " (i.e. the word of God)

Phil.2:1 ".. fellowship of the Spirit .. " (KJV)
1 **Thes.** 5:19 ".. 'Do not quench the Spirit' .. "
1 **Tim.**4:1 ".. in later times .. doctrines of demons .. "
2 **Tim.**1:6 ".. rekindle the gift .. "
Titus 3:5 ".. renewal (reviving) in the Holy Spirit .. "
Heb.9:8 ".. the Holy Spirit indicates .. the way into the
sanctuary .. "
1 **Peter** 4:14 ".. if you are reproached .. "
Jude 20 ".. pray in the Holy Spirit .. "
Rev.3:22 ".. let him hear what the Spirit says .. "

The final command.
Eph.5:18 ".. Be filled with the Spirit .. " i.e. go on being
filled.

26: THE HOLY SPIRIT—The Fullness

This study is to do with the parting words of Christ to His disciples before He ascended to heaven. He told them to "wait for the promise of the Father", and promised that "before many days you shall be baptized with the Holy Spirit." When this did happen "they were all filled with the Holy Spirit."

"We long for 'Revival', an altogether supernatural visitation of the Holy Spirit in the Church, and meanwhile for a deeper, richer, fuller experience of the Holy Spirit in our own lives." (John R. W. Stott, *The Baptism and Fullness of the Holy Spirit*, p.5.)

Christ said—"I came that they may have life,
and have it abundantly" (John 10:10).

Our Lord's promise and the fulfilment.
John 14:16 " . . 'I will pray the Father, and he will give you' . . "
John 14:18 " . . 'I will come to you' . . "
Acts 1:4 " . . 'wait for the promise of the Father' . . "
Acts 1:5 " . . 'be baptized with the Holy Spirit' . . "
Acts 1:8 " . . 'you shall receive power ' . . "
Acts 2:4 " . . they were all filled . . "
Acts 4:8 " . . Then Peter, filled . . "

Paul's exhortation " . . be filled with the Spirit . . " (Eph.5:18) comes to every believer and should be the norm in the experience of each one. There is one baptism, but many fillings.

The full meaning of the words " . . be filled " is brought out by studying the grammatical sense of the original Greek which is:
in the *imperative* tense, like a command,
in the *passive* mood, that is to say it is something that we cannot do ourselves, but that God must do for us,
in the *present continuous* tense, that is to say "go on being filled" or "be being filled".

It is a definite experience, and will be shown by the witness of life and testimony.
Acts 8:15 " . . prayed . . they might receive the Holy Spirit . . "
Acts 19:2 " . . 'Did you receive the Holy Spirit?' . . "
1 Cor.12:13 " . . by one Spirit we were all baptized into one body . . "
John 1:16 " . . from his fullness have we all received . . "

The fullness of the Spirit is evident in the believer's life by the presence of **nine fruits of the Spirit,** sometimes called "the nine graces", evidences of a Christ-like life. The Greek word for "the fruit" is *"karpos"*, a *singular* word, which includes all the attributes.
John 15:8 " . . that you bear much fruit . . " our Lord's own purpose for His disciples.
Gal.5:22, 23 " . . But the fruit of the Spirit is **love, joy, peace, patience, kindness, goodness, faithfulness, gentleness, self-control** . . "—a fruit like a bunch of grapes, all given together.

There are also a number of gifts of the Spirit, nine mentioned in I Cor. 12, which are given individually, or personally, that is to say to different individuals in the community known as "the body of Christ". (About twenty gifts in all are mentioned in the five N.T. lists).

> I Cor.12:7 " .. each man is given his gift .. "(JBP)
> I Cor.12:8 " .. To one .. wisdsom, and to another .. knowledge.."
> I Cor.12:9 " .. faith .. gifts of healing .."
> I Cor.12:10 " .. miracles .. prophecy .. to distinguish between spirits .. tongues .. interpretation of tongues .. "
> I Cor.12:11 " .. who apportions to each one individually as he wills .. "

When is the Fullness experienced?—When we obey.

> Is.1:19 " .. If you are willing and obedient, you shall eat the good of the land .. "
> Acts 5:32 " .. the Holy Spirit .. given to those who obey him .. "

For what purpose was the Fullness of the Spirit given? It is primarily given for power for witness, testimony, preaching the Gospel, for wisdom, healing, "helps" of all kinds, and for joyfulness.

> Acts 1:8 " .. you shall receive power .. "
> Acts 4:31 " .. spoke the word .. with boldness .. "
> Acts 6:3 " .. full of the Spirit and of wisdom .. "
> John 14:26 " .. the Holy Spirit .. will teach you .. "
> I Cor.12:7 " .. for the common good .. "
> I Cor.12:28 " .. healers, helpers, administrators .. "
> Eph.5:18, 19 " .. singing and making melody .. "
> I Pet.4:10 " .. employ it for one another .. "

What are the conditions for the continuing of Fullness? We must long for, and hunger for this "Continuous Fullness" which results in "Continuous Revival", because " .. without (holiness) no one will see the Lord." (Heb.12:14.) John in his first epistle gives us the key. "If we say we have no sin, we deceive ourselves, and the truth is not in us. If we confess our sins, he is faithful .. " (1 John 1:8, 9).

> 2 Chron.7:14 " .. if my people .. humble themselves .. "
> Ps.51:17 " .. a broken and contrite heart .. "
> Is.57:15 " .. to revive the heart of the contrite .. "

There are four warnings against losing the Fullness of the Spirit— Lie not! Resist not! Grieve not! Quench not!

> Acts 5:3 " .. why .. lie to the Holy Spirit .. " (Ananias)
> Acts 7:51 " .. you always resist .. "
> Eph.4:30 " .. do not grieve the Holy Spirit .. "
> I Thes.5:19 " .. Do not quench the Spirit .. "

Devotional note on the Water of Life, and the filling of men's hearts (cups) with the Holy Spirit to overflowing:

Commenting on the occasion of the Feast of Tabernacles when Jesus made His strong appeal—"If any one thirst, let him come to me and drink" (John 7:37), John Stott makes this observation: "It was the last day of the Feast of Tabernacles .. every morning a solemn procession, headed by a priest carrying a golden pitcher, went to fetch water from the Pool of Siloam . . (J.R.W.S. *Ibid.*, p.21).

Jesus may have witnessed this ceremony at that time when He called out those striking words. John in his Gospel makes it very clear that Christ was referring to the outpouring of the Holy Spirit, and that the Spirit would flow out from our innermost lives.

Was Christ referring to the cleansing of our hearts from sin when He drank to the dregs the cup of bitterness in Gethsemane, and died for the world? He can fill only cleansed cups. (Matt.20:22; 26:36–42; John 19:30).

27: SANCTIFICATION—The Highway of Holiness

The vital doctrine of sanctification means the 'setting apart" of a life, by the Holy Spirit, for God. The words used for sanctification, in Hebrew *qodesh*, in Greek *hagios*, and in Latin *sanctus*, may also refer to places, days, or objects used for worship. The "personal holiness" that God expects of *every* saved person is the key that unlocks the floodgates of Revival and "without which no one will see the Lord." (Heb.12:14). It is essential for the walk on the Highway. "By sanctification God places us in the light that He is in." Oswald Chambers.

In the Old Testament God teaches the meaning of holiness:—the seventh day was to be set apart as holy—Mount Sinai, the High Priest's garments, the altar of sacrifice, the sin-offering, a man's house, the field of battle, silver and gold, all the people, all the furniture of the Temple, Mount Zion, and so on.

Gen.2:3 ".. blessed the seventh day .."
Ex.19:23 ".. Mount Sinai .. consecrate it .."
Ex.28:1-3 ".. holy garments for Aaron .." (KJV)
Ex.29:37, 42 ".. the altar shall be most holy .. I will .. speak there to you .."
Lev.27:14 ".. a man dedicates his house to be holy .."
Josh.5:15 ".. the place .. is holy .."
Josh.6:19 ".. all silver and gold .. are sacred .."
Josh.7:13 ".. Sanctify yourselves .."
1 Kings 7:51 ".. the things .. David .. had dedicated .."
Ps.2:6 ".. on Zion, my holy hill .."

In the New Testament the believer is "set apart" at conversion and in so far as he is willing, he is made holy by the Holy Spirit. Christ prayed for His followers that they would be sanctified.

Mark 1:17 ".. follow me, and I will make you .."
John 17:17 ".. Sanctify them .."
1 Cor.6:19 ".. your body is a temple of the Holy Spirit .."
Eph.1:4 ".. holy and blameless before him .."
Eph.2:21 ".. into a holy temple .."
Eph.5:26 ".. sanctify her having cleansed her .."
Col.3:12 ".. holy and beloved .."
1 Thes.5:23 ".. spirit and soul and body .."
Heb.2:11 ".. he who sanctifies .."
Heb.10:10 ".. through the offering of ..Jesus Christ .."
Heb.10:14 ".. perfected .. those who are sanctified .."

It can be said that there are stages of Holiness, the initial Sanctification when the Holy Spirit is given at conversion, followed by other deeper and fuller Sanctification, when the Spirit is allowed full control following more repentance and cleansing in the Blood of Jesus, with a broken and contrite heart. The teaching that there is only one "second blessing" is erroneous. We must go on being sanctified and filled, many times as Paul says, "Go on being filled .." (Eph.5:18).

John 2:13-17 .. The cleansing of the temple.

1 Cor.3:16 " . . you are God's temple . . "
2 Cor.7:1 " . . from every defilement . . "
2 Tim.2:21 " . . a vessel for noble use . . "
Heb.4:16 " . Let us then with confidence draw near . . "
Heb.12:15 " . . that no 'root of bitterness' . . "
Rom.10:4 " . . For Christ means the end of the struggle . . " (JBP)

The Highway of Holiness. All those who have entered into the experience of sanctification or real brokenness, find themselves walking along the Highway of Holiness with the Lord Jesus, the "author and finisher of our faith". They are those who know "the sinner's place" at Calvary, and who are "resting" in the daily cleansing of the Precious Blood.

Is.35:8 " . . a highway shall be there . . Called the Holy Way . . "
Is.35:8 " . . the unclean shall not pass over it . . "
Is.35:8 " . . the wayfaring men . . shall not err therein . . " (KJV)
Is.35:9 " . . the redeemed shall walk there . . "
Is.35:10 " . . with singing: everlasting joy . . "
Is.35:10 " . . sorrow and sighing shall flee away . . "
Is.40:31 " . . renew their strength . . run and not be weary . . "
Is.42:3 " . . a bruised reed he will not break . . "
Is.42:6 " . . I have taken you by the hand and kept you . . "
Is.57:15 " . . revive the spirit of the humble . . "
Phil.3:8 " . . that I may gain Christ . . "
Heb.12:2 " . . Jesus the author and finisher of our faith . . " (KJV)

Devotional Note on the Standard of the Highest. We are to "press toward the mark for the prize of the high calling of God in Christ Jesus." Some have seen in this the picture of Christ going on ahead holding up His banner. His standard of the "Highest"; with the Holy Spirit calling every action to measure up to that standard of true Holiness—our words, our thoughts, life, our homes, our money, and our business. Finney wrote, "What shall we do to lift up the standard (of Revival) to move this entire nation . . (U.S.A.)?".

Rom.13:13 " . . walk honestly . . " (KJV)
Eph.5:2 " . . walk in love . . "
Col.2:6 " . . so walk ye in him . . " (KJV)
1 John 1:7 " . . walk in the light . . "

Aids to maintain the Sanctified Life.
1. A disciplined time must be set apart each day (the quiet time) for prayer and Bible study.
2. Enjoy being in a challenging fellowship (cf. The Upper Room).
3. Instant obedience to the voice of the Holy Spirit through the Word, the Conscience.
4. Note:
   a. that the *Eradication theory* of Sanctification (that the evil principle of sin has been rooted out) is unscriptural.
   b. that the *Suppression theory* (cf. we must crucify the old man) leads to perpetual struggle.
   c. the *Counteraction theory* as above, that the evil nature is "rendered helpless" (Gr. *katargeo*) as long as we continually return to the Cross for cleansing and renewal when temptation comes.

28: LOVE—The Love of God

Love in its highest ethical sense is the very nature of God. This greatest Christian virtue is described in Scripture by listing its attributes. It comes from God and it is only seen when man's relationship with man (with Him) are right. The highest expression of God's love was seen in the Lord Jesus, and poured out on the cross at Calvary, and bequeathed to man by God through the Holy Spirit. It is the love that even loves one's enemies.

A special word in Greek is used, *agape*, which can be translated as "brotherly love" (OED). The old word "charity" is used in KJV.

In the Old Testament the love of God began to be revealed to man, and he had to love God in return. It was foreshadowed in the sacrifices, in the vicarious suffering of the lambs.

Lev.19:18 " . . you shall love your neighbour . . "
Deut.6:5 " . . you shall love the Lord your God . . "
Deut.10:12 " . . to fear . . to walk . . to love . . "
2 Sam.7:8, 14 " . . Thus says the Lord . . I will be his father . . "
2 Sam.12:24 " . . the Lord loved him . . "
Ps.18:1 " . . I love thee, O Lord . . "
Ps.89:26 " . . Thou art my father . . "
Ps.23 . . The caring Shepherd. (NEB)
Prov.10:12 " . . love covers all offences . . "
Prov.17:17 " . . friend loves at all times . . "
Prov.27:5, 6 . . Only love can challenge. Cf. Matt.18:15
Is.43:4 " . . I love you . . "
Is.66:13 " . . I will comfort you . . "
Jer.31:3 " . . with an everlasting love . . "
Hos.11:1–4 . . God said of Israel, " . . I loved him . . "

In the New Testament Christ came to show to the world the love of God, to crown it with His death upon the cross. The word *agape* comes into its own and is used ninety-five times out of a hundred by the Septuagint translation.

Matt.5:44 " . . I say . . Love your enemies . . "
Mark 1:41 " . . moved with pity . . "
Luke 19:41 " . . saw the city he wept over it . . "
John 3:16 " . . God so loved the world . . "
John 13:34 " . . love one another; even as I have loved you . . "
John 13:35 " . . my disciples, if you have love for one another . . "
Rom.5:8 " . . while we were yet sinners . . "
Rom.13:8 " . . Owe no one anything, except to love one another . . "
2 Cor.5:14 " . . the love of Christ controls us . . "
Gal.2:20 " . . the Son of God, who loved me . . "
Gal.5:22 " . . The fruit of the spirit is love . . "
Eph.5:2 " . . walk in love . . "
Col.3:13, 14 " . . Forbearing . . forgiving each other . . "
James 2:8–12 " . . the royal law . . the law of liberty . . "
1 Peter 3:8 . . In the home; " . . have unity . . love of the brethren . . "

I Peter 4:8 ".. above all hold unfailing your love for one another .."
I John 4:8–10 .. The supreme expression of God's love on Calvary.

John, the apostle of love, writes about "perfect love".
I John 4:18 ".. perfect love casts out fear .."
I John 4:7–21, 5:1–3 ".. God is love .."

Paul, in a masterpiece of literature, describes the Holy Spirit's characteristics of the Love of God as seen in a truly Christlike life.

(The first quotation from I Corinthians 13 in each case is taken from the RSV, with alternative quotes from other versions, giving further light.)

I Cor. 13:4a ".. Love is patient .."
        —slow to lose patience. (JBP)
13:4b ".. and kind .."
        —looks for a way of being constructive. (JBP)
13:4c ".. love is not jealous .."
        —charity envieth not. (KJV)
13:4d ".. or boastful .."
        —not puffed up. (KJV)
13:5a ".. it is not arrogant .."
13:5b ".. or rude .."
        —doth not behave itself unseemly. (KJV)
13:5c ".. does not insist on its own way .."
13:5d ".. it is not irritable .."
        —it is not touchy. (JBP)
13:5e ".. or resentful .."
        —keeps no score of wrongs. (NEB)
13:6a ".. it does not rejoice at wrong .."
        —not happy with evil. (TEV)
13:6b ".. but rejoices in the right .."
13.7a ".. Love bears all things .."
        —no limit to its endurance. (JBP)
13:7b ".. believes all things .."
        —love never gives up. (TEV)
13:7c ".. hopes all things .."
        —no fading of its hope. (JBP)
13:7d ".. endures all things .."
        —can outlast. (JBP)
13:8 ".. Love never ends .."
        —love is eternal. (TEV)
13:13 ".. So faith, hope, love abide, these three; but the greatest of these is love .."

The final plea.
    I Cor.14:1 ".. Make love your aim .."

29: LIGHT—Life in the Light

The concept of Light emerges in Scripture with God's command, "Let there be light" (Gen.1:3). Without light on the earth there could be no life. It is possible to build up an entire theological doctrine on the subject of light. In the physical world we have the contrasts of light and darkness, day and night, knowledge and ignorance and life and death. From these arise the ethical analogies of good and evil and of spiritual life and death.

Light represents the Holiness of God—".. God is light.." (1 John 1:5) and all was summed up in the majestic words of Christ—".. 'I am the light of the world.. the light of life.'.." (John 8:12).

In the Old Testament God uses light and fire to demonstrate His presence, to accompany His messages, and to light up man's way.

Gen.1:3 ".. 'Let there be light'.."
Ex.3:1-3 ".. in a flame of fire.."
Ex.13:21 ".. in a pillar of fire.."
Ex.24:16 ".. The glory of the Lord settled.."
Num.6:25 ".. make his face to shine.."
1 Kings 8:11 ".. the glory.. filled the house of the Lord.."
Ps.4:6 ".. the light of thy countenance.."
Ps.90:8 ".. our secret sins in the light.."
Ps.119:105 ".. a light to my path.."
Is.2:5 ".. walk in the light of the Lord.."
Is.50:10 ".. walks in darkness.."
Is.50:11 .. false light ".. the light of your fire.."
Hab.3:3, 4 ".. His brightness was like the light.."

In the New Testament Christ identifies Himself with the Old Testament light of God and with the "Shekinah" glory. He now *is* the Light personified, comes to commune with man, and to light up his way. Without Him is darkness.

Matt.17:2 .. At the Transfiguration—".. his face shone like the sun.."
Matt.27:45 .. At the Crucifixion—".. there was darkness.."
Luke 1:79 ".. to give light.. in darkness.."
Luke 2:32 ".. A light to lighten the Gentiles.." (KJV)
John 1:4 ".. the light of men.."
John 1:14 ".. we have beheld his glory.."
John 3:19-21 ".. light has come.. men loved darkness rather than light.."
John 8:12 ".. 'the light of life'.."
John 9:5 ".. 'I am the light of the world'.."
Acts 2:3 ".. tongues as of fire.."
Acts 9:3 ".. a light from heaven.."
2 Cor.4:4 ".. the light of the gospel.."
Rev.21:23 ".. the glory of God is its light, and its lamp is the Lamb.."

The Christian life is a pilgrimage, we are to walk as children of light.

Christ's presence brings awareness of sin, and immediate confession and forgiveness keeps fellowship unbroken for those who walk in His light.

Matt.5:14 " . . 'You are the light of the world' . . "
Matt.5:16 " . . 'Let your light so shine' . . "
Rom.13:12 " . . the armour of light . . "
Eph.5:8 " . . you are light in the Lord . . "
Eph. 5:14 " . . 'Christ shall give you light' . . "
1 John 1:1 " . . heard . . seen . . looked upon and touched . . "
1 John 1:7a " . . if we walk in the light, as he is in the light, we have fellowship . . "
1 John 1:7b " . . the blood of Jesus his Son cleanses (Gr. goes on cleansing) us from all sin . . "
1 John 2:6 " . . walk in the same way in which he walked . . "
1 John 2:8 " . . the true light is already shining . . "

Light and Dark along life's way. The Holy Spirit reveals the cause of darkness through conscience, warning us when we have gone wrong, like an umpire. Paul uses the Greek word for umpire when he writes of the peace of Christ *ruling* in our hearts (Col.3:15).

John 12:35 " . . 'Walk while you have the light' . . "
" . . 'he who walks in the darkness does not know' . . "
John 12:36 " . . 'become sons of light' . . "
2 Cor.4:6 " . . 'Let light shine out of darkness' . . "
2 Cor.6:14 " . . what fellowship has light with darkness ? . . "
1 John 2:9-11 " . . hates his brother . . walks in the darkness . . "

Devotional Study.

John seems to imply that immediately there is any infringement of love we begin to get into the dark. With Love come all its attibutes described in 1 Cor.13:4-7. Love is patient, kind, not jealous, not boastful, not arrogant, not irritable or resentful. With Hate come all *its* attributes, which are the opposites of the above. Hate is impatient, unkind, jealous, boastful, arrogant, irritable and resentful.

John is more explicit when he writes of lack of love as hate.

1 John 2:9 " . . He who says he is in the light and **hates** his brother is in the darkness still . . "

As we seek to understand the causes of spiritual darkness we can see all the sins that come under the heading of hate.

He who says he is in the light and is jealous of—is rude to—is dishonest with—is cruel to—is lustful with—or lies to his brother, and he who avoids—bluffs—sneers at—snubs or despises his brother **is in darkness.**

"If we say we have no sin, we deceive ourselves . . " (1 John 1:8).

Gen.3:9 " . . the Lord God called to the man (Adam) . . 'Where are you?' . . "
James 5:16 " . . confess your sins to one another . . "
1 John 1:9 " . . If we confess our sins, he . . will forgive our sins and cleanse us from all righteousness . . "
1 Peter 2:9 " . . But you are a chosen race . . called . . out of darkness into his **marvellous light** . . "
1 John 1:5 " . . God is light and in him is no darkness at all . . "

30: FELLOWSHIP—Oneness

At the beginning of the Bible we find God stating His plan for man—"It is not good that man should be alone" (Gen.2:18). He created them male and female, and the first fellowship was to be with God and with one another. The Bible uses a Greek word, *koinonia*, to describe this kind of fellowship and this word is used twenty times in the New Testament. It means "sharing in something with someone", and the Latin equivalent is *communio*. In history true fellowship always comes to life in times of revival and awakening, but when the Church grows cold it withers away and seems to be forgotten. After Pentecost it was the love of Jesus seen and lived in the lives of Christians.

In the Old Testament. Satan attacks the first God-given Fellowship, dividing man from God, and man from his companion, and bringing in fear, hiding and blaming. But God came to restore fellowship, calling to Adam .. "Where art thou?" (KJV).

Gen.3:8-13 " .. 'I was afraid .. I hid myself' .. "
Gen.5:24 " .. walked with God .. "
Gen.12:1 " .. God chose a man, a family, and a nation of twelve tribes."
Ex.25:22 " .. And there .. I will commune with thee .. " (KJV)
Lev.19:18 " .. love your neighbour .. "
Deut.6:5 " .. love the Lord your God .. "
Jer.32:39 " .. 'one heart and one way' .. "
Amos 3:3 " .. Can two walk together, except .. " (KJV)
Mal.3:16 " .. spoke with one another .. "
James 2:23 " .. 'Abraham' .. the friend of God .. "

In the New Testament. Although the nation of Israel failed all down the ages individuals found peace with God through sins forgiven, and fellowship restored. Then Christ Himself came and called out twelve disciples with whom He lived in close fellowship for three years. After He died, oneness, which is true fellowship, was the outcome of the fullness of the Holy Spirit (2 Cor.13:14), and He promised that—"where two or three are gathered in my name, there am I in the midst of them" (Matt.18:20).

Matt.10:1 " .. he called to him his twelve disciples .. "
Mark 6:7 " .. two by two .. "
John 13:34 " .. that you love one another .. "
John 17:11, 22 " .. that they may be one .. "
John 17:22 " .. The glory .. I have given to them .. "
2 Cor.13:14 " .. the fellowship of the Holy Spirit .. "

True fellowship is learned at the cross, because it is there that forgiveness is found, and that is where men enter into "the fellowship of His sufferings." That is where the fullness of the Spirit is received.

Acts 1:4 " .. wait for the promise .. "
Acts 2:3 " .. on each one of them .. "
Acts 2:42 " .. the apostles' teaching and fellowship .. "
Acts 8:4 " .. scattered .. preaching the word .. "
Acts 4:13 " .. they recognised that they had been with Jesus .. "

1 Cor.12:12 ff " . . the body is one . . "
Phil.3:10 " . . the fellowship of his sufferings . . " (KJV)

The upper room Fellowship. It seems that the over-confident Peter was humbled, Thomas no longer doubted, Nicodemus at the cross came right out, John learned about deeper love—the *agape*—the family of Jesus became one; they shared their things, open-ness was natural and the fellowship grew.

Acts 2:42 " . . they devoted themselves to . . fellowship . . "
1 Cor.1:9 " . . called into the fellowship . ."
2 Cor.8:3 . . giving— " . . according to their means . . "
2 Cor.8:23 . . team-work— " . . my partner and fellow worker . . "
2 Cor.6:11 . . frank speaking— "we are hiding nothing from you" (JBP)
Gal.2:9 . . out of controversy— " . . the right hand of
    fellowship . . "
Gal.6:1 . . backsliders— " . . restore him in a spirit of gentleness . ."
Eph.4:26 . . anger— " . . Never go to bed angry . . " (JBP)
Philemon 6 . . sharing— " . . the sharing of your faith . . "
James 5:16 . . fellowship of sinners— " . . confess your sins to
    one another . . "
1 Pet.4:13 . . suffering— " . . partakers of Christ's sufferings . . "
(KJV)

The secret of Fellowship. John says, We want you to be with us in this—in this fellowship with God the Father, and Jesus Christ his Son. We must write and tell you about it. . . . Here, then, is the message we heard Him give. GOD IS LIGHT . . . if we really are living in the same light . . . then we have true fellowship with each other, and the blood which He shed for us keeps us clean from any and every sin" (1 John 1:3-7, JBP).

1 John 1:1 " . . which we have heard . . seen . . touched . . "
1 John 1:3a " . . that you may have fellowship with us . . "
1 John 1:3b " . . and with his Son Jesus Christ . . "
1 John 1:7 " . . cleanses us (Gr. continuously) from all sin . . " .
1 John 1:8 . . There is no 'sinless perfection'.
1 John 1:9 . . Immediate repentance restores the fellowship.

The first Christian Fellowships met in their homes. They gathered for the simplest form of worship—for prayer, praise, teaching and testimony. This can be called "the Fellowship Meeting", and it ended often, as Christ had told them, with the remembering of His death in the breaking of bread and the sharing of the cup. This act of fellowship was obviously intended for those who were His followers and in deep fellowship.
    The House Groups and Bible Study Groups that are springing up all over the Christian world today are in this tradition, as the wind of the Holy Spirit blows again in revival.

Acts 1:13 " . . they went up to the upper room . . "
Acts 2:42 " . . the apostles' teaching and fellowship . . "
Acts 2:46 " . . breaking bread in their homes . . "
Acts 5:42 " . . teaching and preaching . . "
1 Cor.12:12 " . . the body is one . . many members . . "
2 Cor.6:14 " . . not unequally yoked . . " (KJV)
Rev.22:2 " . . for the healing of the nations . . "

Some practical notes

John Wesley (in his *Journal*, 8th March 1747) described fellowship as " a company of men . . seeking the power of godliness; united in order to pray together, to receive the word of exhortation, and to watch over one another in love."

For fellowship meetings seats may be arranged in a wide circle, as a reminder of oneness. In preparation those taking part may ask themselves— Do I really want to be right with God? Do I really want to be open with the fellowship? Am I willing to be be helped by any member? Am I willing to deal lovingly with any wrong in the fellowship?

31: LAW—Works

By law is meant, the God-given age that existed in the world prior to the death of Christ. Law is in contrast to grace, e.g., law demands righteousness—grace bestows it.

The ten commandments written by the hand of God have been called "a monument more imperishable than the pyramids".

In the Old Testament, righteousness was granted by God on the condition of obedience to the Law accompanied by repentance and faith. But under Law man failed, because he tried to obtain righteousness by fulfilling the Law only, but "not of faith". Law was the "schoolmaster". Law concluded "all under sin".

Ex.20:1–26 " . . you shall have no other gods before me . . "
Ex.24:12 " . . Come up to me on the mountain . . "
Ex.31:18 " . . tables of stone written with the finger of God . . "
Deut.6:5–9 " . . love the Lord your God . . "
Ps.1:2 " . . his delight is in the law . . "
Ps.19:7, 8 " . . is perfect . . is sure . . are right . . is pure . . is clean . . are true . . more to be desired . . than gold . . "
Ps.37:31 " . . The law of his God is in his heart . . "
Ps.40:8 " . . I delight to do thy will . . " (David)
Ps.119:1 . . "Blessed . . who walk in the law . . "

Under Law man failed. The Old Testament said "DO!" The New Testament says "DONE!"

Is.1:13–18 " . . bring no more vain offerings . . "
Is.5:24 " . . They have rejected the law . . "
Dan.9:8–13 " . . To us . ., O Lord, belongs confusion of face . . "

In the New Testament we find how Christ came to complete the dispensation of Law, and to provide a new way—the way of grace.

Matt.5:17 " . . Think not that I have come to abolish the law . . "
Matt.22:36 " . . Teacher, which is the great commandment? . . "
Matt.22:37 . . Jesus said " . . You shall love . . "
John 1:17 " . . Law . . Moses . . grace . . Jesus Christ . . "
Acts 13:39 " . . By him, everyone that believes . . "
Acts 15:5, 10, 11, 28 . . The Circumcision controversy.
Rom.3:20 " . . through the law comes knowledge of sin . . "
Rom.8:3, 4 " . . For God . . sending his own Son . . "
Rom.10:4 " . . Christ means the end of the struggle for righteousness . . " (Phillips)
Gal.3:11, 24 " . . that we might be justified by faith . . "— (Luther's basic reformation text)
Phil.3:3 " . . put no confidence in the flesh . . "

The freedom of grace has been bought with the blood of Christ. Therefore any Christians who go back to Law in any form are under the judgment of God.

Gal.3:10 " . . under a curse . . "
Gal.5:2 " . . Christ will be of no advantage to you . . "

32: GRACE—The unmerited love of God

Grace means, in the Bible, the unmerited favour of God, or "the kindness and love of God our Saviour toward men . . not by works of righteousness which we have done" (KJV). Gr. *charis* = grace. Grace is in contrast to Law, and to works. Under law, God demands righteousness from man; under grace, He gives righteousness to man. In popular speech it means charm, loveliness, attractiveness—Christ was full of grace, (Luke 4:22) and "Grace and truth came through Jesus Christ."

The great themes of scripture, forgiveness, salvation, regeneration, repentance, and love are sometimes called "grace-words" because they are bound up with the grace of God.

The **present age of grace** began in the world with the death and resurrection of Christ. Now, this precious gift of grace is given to all believers, and available to all men. A Christ-like man is a gracious man (2 Tim.2:1).

Grace is a synonym of the gracious gifts of the Holy Spirit (Heb.10:29).

John 1:17 " . . law . . through Moses; grace . . through Jesus . . "
John 1:12, 13 " . . he gave power to become . . "
John 3:36 " . . believes in the Son has . . "
Rom.3:24-27 " . . they are justified by his grace as a gift . . "
Rom.5:2, 15-21 " . . access to this grace . . "
Rom.6:14 " . . not under law but under grace . . "
2 Cor.6:1-3 " . . the grace of God in vain . . "
2 Cor.8:9 " . . you know the grace . . "
Gal.1:3-15 " . . grace and peace . . "—a greeting and benediction.
Gal.2:20 " . . not I but Christ . . " (KJV)
Gal.5:4 " . . fallen away from grace . . "
Titus 3:4, 5 " . . the goodness and loving kindness of God . . "

Law demands—grace gives, "Thou shalt not" gives place to "Thou shalt . . ". "Law blesses the good—grace saves the bad."

Deut.28:1-9 " . . if you obey . . blessed shall you be . . "
John 3:16 " . . that he gave . . "
Rom.8:3 " . . what the law . . could not do . . "
Rom.10:4-10 " . . Christ is the end of the law . . "
Phil.3:9 " . . based on law . . "
Heb.7:19 " . . the law made nothing perfect . . "
Ex.19:5 ⎫
Eph.2:8, 9 ⎭ " . . if you will obey my voice . . not because of works . . "

The Holy Spirit helps us to grow in grace.

2 Cor.12:9 " . . My grace is sufficient for you . . "
Phil.4:6 " . . Have no anxiety about anything . . "
Heb.4:16 " . . draw near to the throne of grace . . "
Jas.4:6 " . . He (the Holy Spirit) gives more grace . . "
1 Pet.5:5 " . . God . . gives grace to the humble . . " grace . . "
1 Pet.5:10 " . . **God of all grace** . . "

Under Law the world failed, and ended by crucifying Christ. Similarly under grace this age will end in apostasy, and the judgments that the Bible predicts. But it is man who fails, not God's plan of grace.

2 Thess.2:11, 12 " . . strong delusion . . "
2 Tim.3:1–8 " . . perilous times shall come . . " (KJV)
2 Pet.2:1 " . . destructive heresies . . "
1 John 4:1–3 " . . false prophets . . "
Jude 4, 8, 11–13,16 " . . pervert the grace of our God . . "
Rev.3:17 " . . wretched, pitiable, poor, blind . . "

The freedom and simplicity of grace is God's final plan of salvation for the world. Any other gospel is "anathema."

Gal.1:6–9 " . . let him be accursed . . "
cf. John 10:1 " . . but climbs in by another way . . "

A special note on the means of grace

By this is meant the God-given channels through which blessing comes to our souls. But the blessing, i.e. His grace, remains unchanged. It is always the same 'unmerited favour' of God towards man. There are NOT special types of grace. The following are the principal means of grace. The order given here is not necessarily the order of importance.

1. PRAYER—Especially our quiet times with God—This is the basis of all other means of grace because it is the key to our personal relationship to Christ.

Heb.4:16 " . . with confidence . . find grace . . "

2. BIBLE STUDY—The Bible itself is a vital means of grace. By it God convicts, saves, sanctifies and guides. It is His very voice speaking to us.

2 Tim.3:15 " . . The sacred writings . . to instruct you for salvation . . "

3. WITNESS—God uses the ministry and witness of His own children through teaching and preaching, to bring others to Christ by the spoken word, by song, or by life. It has been called "truth expressed by personality". We must realise that Christ calls every Christian man and woman to witness to Him in some way or other, but also in all bodies of the Christian church, God sets aside certain people to give whole-time service.

Rom.10:10 " . . confesses with his lips and so is saved . . "

4. WORSHIP—Worship may be in the home, or in any congregation of believers, cf., "Where two or three are gather together in my name there am I in the midst." Neglect of this means of grace is generally the result of neglect of the preceding three (cf. Heb.10:25).

Heb.10:25 " . . neglecting to meet together . . "

5. BAPTISM—This and the Holy Communion, are sometimes called sacraments (Lat. *sacramenta*). They differ from the preceding four in that they were sacred ordinances commissioned by Christ Himself.

Mark 16:16 " . . he who believes and is baptised . . "

6. THE LORD'S SUPPER—Of the so-called sacraments, most Protestant churches have retained only two, Baptism and the Lord's Supper. Great confusion and abuse has grown up around the word sacrament owing to sacerdotal errors. A sacrament is symbolism, "an outward visible sign of an inward and spiritual grace." Error arose from the teaching that the priest has the power and prerogative to administer grace, *ex opere operato* (Lat.) by the work performed.

Finally it must be borne in mind that no means of grace is effectual apart from the seeker's personal faith in Jesus Christ.

33: APOSTASY—"falling away"

The word "Apostasy" is derived from the Greek word *apostasia*, meaning "withdrawal" or "falling away", and has a bad sense in Church history. There is a bias in human nature towards sin, which comes out continually in the Old and New Testaments. Apostasy is non-denominational, that is to say, it is something that attacks all God's people and all Christian bodies. Its onset is insidious, its end is terrible, if there is no repentance. Apostates depart from the faith, but not all from outward profession of Christianity. We are warned in the New Testament that it will be a sign of the last days.

Phil.3:18 " . . enemies of the cross . . "
2 Thes.2:3 " . . except there come a falling away . . " (KJV)
2 Tim.2:26 " . . from the snare of the devil . . "
2 Tim.3:1 " . . in the last days there will come times of stress . . "
2 Tim.3:2 " . . proud, arrogant, abusive . . "
2 Pet.2:1 " . . false teachers . . destructive heresies . . "
Jude 4 " . . admission . . secretly gained . . "
Jude 11 " . . walk in the way of Cain . . "

What is the first stage of "falling away"? Jude calls it *"the way of Cain"*. This seems to imply that the religious natural man, who outwardly believes in God, and in religious observances, can fail. Cain it appears rejected the forgiveness of his sin by the shedding of blood of an innocent animal, and presented God with the works of his own hands. Abel returned guilt-free and carefree after knowing that his sins had been "covered" by the blood of his sacrifice. This tended to make his elder brother more morose and jealous, till one day in a fit of anger he murdered him.

What does it mean in our day? People "fall away" when they call salvation through the blood of Christ "a shambles", and "old-fashioned", and try to find "another way", through their intellect and reason; or when we trust to our religious zeal and goodness, while sin remains unsurrendered in our hearts. Individuals and whole Christian communities can travel down this road. Moses and the prophets warned Israel; Christ and the writers of the N.T. have warned us. Jude says, " . . it became urgently necessary to write at once and appeal to you to join the struggle in defence of the faith, the faith which God entrusted to his people once and for all." (NEB)

Jude 3 " . . the faith . . once . . delivered . . "
Jude 4 " . . admission . . secretly gained . . "
Heb.11:4 ⎱ " . . Abel offered to God a more acceptable
Gen.4:1–5 ⎰ sacrifice . . "
Gen.4:6, 8 . . Anger and murder.
Gal.1:6 . . Like Cain they tried to find " . . a different gospel . . "
Gal.2:11–14 . . A gospel of "works" (circumcision) which is law not grace.
Gal.3:1 ⎱ " . . O foolish Galatians: Who has bewitched you . . "
Acts 15:1 ⎰
2 Cor.11:3 " . . as the serpent deceived Eve . . "
Col.2:16 " . . let no one pass judgment . . "

What is the second stage of "falling away"? Jude calls it *"the error of Balaam"*. This follows quickly on the way of Cain. Like many religious men who have lost their way and God's way of the cross, Balaam (Num.22-27) advises King Balak to defeat Israel, by encouraging forbidden intermarriage (Num.25:1-3). Balaam (Num. 31:16) "caused Israel to sin". Committees, Church Councils, homes that have lost "the way of the cross", often flounder when faced with the underhand methods of the world.

Jude 11 " . . for the sake of gain to Balaam's error . . "
2 Pet.2:15 " . . gone astray; they have followed the way of Balaam . . "
Rev.2:2, 14 " . . I know your works . . the teaching of Balaam . . "
Rev.3:15 " . . neither cold nor hot . . "
2 Cor.11:13-15 " . . false apostles, deceitful workmen . . "
1 Tim.6:5, 10 " . . the love of money is the root of all evils . . "
2 Tim.3:5 " . . holding the form of religion . . "
2 Pet.2:17, 20, 21 " . . again entangled in them . . "

What is the third and final end of "falling away"? The Greek word implies an established state, a sect, a schism, that is built up on error. It becomes located, and so requires a leader, or leaders, literature and rules. Legalism and fear result, and very soon take the place of love and true fellowship. The equal brotherhood becomes divided into priests and laity, the congregation continuing more and more to trust in their "priesthood", ceremonial and outward forms of worship, liturgies, special vocabulary and dress. It is the intrusion of a man-made priesthood into the office of Christ Himself.

All this may be what is meant in "Revelation" by "the deed of the Nikolaitans", from Gr. "*nikao*"—to conquer, and "*laos*", the people, or laity. The "gainsaying of Korah" shows us a man -made priesthood seeking to intrude itself into the divinely appointed priesthood and leadership of Aaron and Moses.

In New Testament times, up to the present day, the Lord Jesus alone is our Great High Priest but spiritual deadness and coldness bring darkness and necessitate a new outpouring of God's Holy Spirit in revival.

In Church history, there has always been "the hidden remnant" who have kept the faith alive, the Pilgrim Church, those who "have not bowed their knee to Baal", the true pietists, some becoming martyrs, those who live very near to the Lord, feeding upon His word, in secret perhaps as some have to do even today. These men and women become sweeter under persecution.

Jude 11 " . . and perish in Korah's rebellion . . "
Ezk. 8:9 " . . see the vile abominations . . "
Ezk.8:14 " . . women weeping for Tammuz . . "
Ezk.8:16 " . . worshipping the sun . . "
Acts. 20:29 " . . fierce wolves . . not sparing the flock . . "
1 Tim.2:5 " . . one mediator between God and men . . "
1 Tim.4:1-3 " . . doctrines of demons . . consciences are seared . . "
Is.1:9 " . . a very small remnant . . " (KJV)
Is.11:16 " . . a highway . . for the remnant . . "
1 Kings 19:18 . . 7,000 not bowed the knee.
Luke 2:38 . . Simeon and Anna looked for the redemption in Jerusalem.
Rev.7:14 " . . washed their robes . . in the Blood of the Lamb . . "

Devotional Note. The story of the Judges shows who were the enemies of the Promised Land and how they had been allowed to come to life, and defeat

God's people. The actual enemies are seen in Josh.3:10. We can give them fanciful names: the Canaanites, "worldliness"; the Hittites, "strife"; the Hivites, "divisions"; the Perizzites, "compromise"; the Girgashites, "jealousy"; the Amorites, "lust"; and the Jebusites, "hate."

Josh.3:10 . . Victory over all their enemies was promised. But—
Josh 24:23 ". . 'put away the foreign gods' . . "
Judges 1:21 ". . Benjamin did not drive out the Jebusites . . "
Judges 1:27–29, 30 ". . Manasseh did not drive out . .
  Ephraim did not . . Zebulun did not . . "
Judges 1:31, 33 . . Neither did Asher or Naphtali drive them out.
Judges 1:34 ". . The Amorites pressed the Danites . . "
Judges 2:1, 2, 4, 5 . . But the angel of the Lord (possibly Christ Himself) came to help them at Bochim, the place of weeping.

34: THE PROBLEM OF PAIN and SUFFERING

In the Bible all suffering, cruelty and pain are shown to be an intrusion into God's creation, which was "very good". But sin entered and with it came enmity, conflict and corruption. The whole world order is "out of gear", which comes from the Fall. The Bible also says that Christ came to deal with this impasse and that He has gone to prepare a "new heaven and a new earth", where "death shall be no more, neither .. mourning, nor crying, nor pain any more .." Isaiah adds that nothing shall "hurt or destroy". But all suffering remains a baffling problem, as the book of Job shows.

What is to be the Christian attitude toward pain and suffering?
Death is inevitable, and so is suffering and disease. When they occur along the pilgrim way, they must be courageously endured by men of faith, knowing that Christ has conquered death and that He can always heal, and that nothing will happen without God's permissive will. Sometimes He allows men to be refined in the fire of testings so as to get the pure gold that will be left.

Rev.21:1 " .. new heaven and a new earth .. "
Gen.3:18 " .. thorns and thistles .. "
Job.1:21-22 " .. 'the Lord has taken away' .. "
Job.5:17, 23:10 " .. 'despise not the chastening' .. "
Matt.26:38 " .. exceeding sorrowful .. " (KJV)
Acts 14:22 " .. through many tribulations .. "
Rom.5:3 " .. produces endurance .. "
2 Cor.7:10 " .. grief produces a repentance .. "
1 Thes.3:2-4 " .. this is to be our lot .. "
2 Tim.3:11, 12 " .. the Lord rescued me .. "
James 1:2, 3 " .. count it all joy .. "
1 Peter 1:6, 7 " .. more precious than gold .. "

The O.T. revealed the suffering Messiah and we can "enter into His sufferings".

Ps.119:67 " .. Before I was afflicted I went astray .. "
Is.63:8, 9 " .. their Saviour .. he was afflicted .. "
Is.53:4 " .. borne our griefs and carried our sorrows .. "
Matt.16:24 " .. let him .. take up his cross and follow me .. "
Rom.8:17 " .. provided we suffer with him .. "
Phil.1:29 " .. but also suffer for his sake .. "
Phil.3:10 " .. and may share his sufferings .. "
1 Pet.1:11 " .. predicting the sufferings of Christ .. "

The "dark nights of the soul".

Ps.23:4 " .. though I walk through the valley of the shadow of death .. "
Ps.40:1 " .. He inclined to me and heard my cry .. "
John 20:16 " .. Jesus said to her, 'Mary' .. "
Heb.12:11 " .. later it yields the .. fruit of righteousness .. "

"Christ won the victory—"O death, where is thy sting?"

God has it in His power to heal all disease and suffering that may come to us, but we must not dictate to Him. He alone knows "the end from the beginning". His only condition is absolute faith and surrender to Him. (see Ch.7:Faith.) Doubt will dim our vision. The crown of life awaits him who overcomes.

Is.35:10 ".. sorrow and sighing shall flee away .."
Is.46:10 ".. the end from the beginning .."
Matt.4:23 ".. healing every disease .."
John 16:33 ".. 'I have overcome the world' .."
1 Cor.15:20 ".. Christ has been raised .."
1 Cor.15:54 ".. 'Death is swallowed up in victory' .."
2 Cor.4:17 .. Paul's thorn in the flesh.
2 Cor.12:7 ".. a thorn was given me in the flesh .."
Rev.2:10 ".. Do not fear what you are about to suffer, ..
Be faithful unto death,
and I will give you the crown of life .."

35: HEALING—Physical and Spiritual

The whole subject of the healing of the body and the soul is bound up with the problem of sin. There are various methods available to us for the relief of disease:—surgery and medicine, prophylaxis and psychotherapy, faith-healing and humanitarian efforts, but no one method is right to the exclusion of the others. In one case instruments are used, in another medicines, in another the cure is best effected through the mind. There is also entrusted to some believers in Christ the divine power of God through the Holy Spirit to heal miraculously, that is suddenly, bearing in mind that it is God and only God who is carrying on the healing process all the time, all over the world, which is part of His creatorial plan.

In the thirty-five books of the Old Testament there are very few instances recorded of miraculous healing, or raising from the dead.

Ex.9:11 " . . boils were upon . . all the Egyptians . . "—the miracle of the protection of the Jews.

Num.21:9 " . . if a serpent bit any man, he would look . . and live . . "

1 Kings 13:6 " . . the king's hand was restored . . " (Jeroboam)

1 Kings 17:22 " . . the soul of the child . . revived . . "

2 Kings 4:34, 35 " . . the child became warm . . "

2 Kings 5:14 " . . his flesh was restored . . " (Naaman)

2 Kings 20:5 " . . I will heal you . . " (Hezekiah)

In the New Testament when Christ returned from the wilderness filled with the Spirit He combined healing with His ministry of preaching.

Matt.4:23 " . . healing every disease and every infirmity . . "

Matt.8:13 " . . healed at that very moment . . "

Matt.8:16 " . . cast out the spirits . . "

Matt.14:14 " . . he had compassion on them . . "

Luke 4:18 " . . The Spirit of the Lord . . recovering of sight to the blind . . "

Luke 4:40 " . . he laid his hands on every one of them and healed them . . "

The Devil who was active in the wilderness continued to oppose Christ's healing ministry through demons. Christ cast them out with a command and by authority.

Matt.17:18 " . . Jesus rebuked him, and the demon came out . . "

Matt.25:41 " . . prepared for the devil and his angels . . "

Mark 1:32 " . . possessed with demons . . "

Mark 1:34 " . . he would not permit the demons to speak . . "

When Christ had risen from the grave He bequeathed to His disciples power to cast out devils, and caring and healing were gifts of the Holy Spirit.

Matt.10:1 " . . he . . gave them authority over unclean spirits . . "

Matt.10:8 " . . heal the sick, raise the dead, cleanse lepers, cast out demons . . "

Luke 10:17 " . . Lord, even the demons are subject to us . . "
Acts 3:6 " . . in the name of Jesus Christ . . walk . . "
1 Cor.12:9 " . . to another gifts of healing . . "

The high calling to follow in Christ's footsteps. It is the greatest privilege in the world. Yet many devoted workers fall short. A whole life given to humanitarian work or to medicine, or to other philanthropic work, will be of no avail to the soul if the heart has not been yielded to Christ.

Sectarian beliefs that God will inevitably cure without the use of modern medicines or surgery, are as foolish as refusing to use any other scientific discoveries. Also the belief that there can be complete freedom from disease, if there is sufficient faith, is as unattainable as sinless perfection. Even the Lord Himself did not heal all diseases in His day.

The miraculous gifts of healing, and other charismatic signs, seem to have been provided at Pentecost to give authority to the preaching of the Gospel, but there are signs today of a new outpouring of the Holy Spirit, perhaps to prepare the world for Christ's near return.

36: DEATH—Physical and Spiritual

Physical death is universal. When a man dies his soul is parted from his physical body. The Bible calls the eternal death of the soul of man "the second death". Spiritual death is the state of the soul of the natural man born in sin, who has not yet been "born again". Man, during his lifetime on earth, must accept or reject Christ, and on this decision his final destiny depends.

The Bible says that sin came into the world through one man and "spread to all men". But there was life and death, seed-time and harvest, everything was beautiful and "very good", in man's first home, so the words "by man came death" must refer to spiritual death, which is a state of eternal separation from God.

Gen.1:31 ".. God saw everything that he had made, and behold, it was very good.."
Gen.3:17, 18 .. But after sin entered, ".. cursed is the ground .. thorns and thistles.."
Rom.5:12 ".. death spread to all men.."
Rom.5:12 ".. sin came into the world through one man.."
Rom. 5:18 ".. condemnation for all men.."
Rom.8:22 ".. the whole creation .. groaning in travail.."
1 Cor.15:21 ".. by man came death.." (KJV)

Universal spiritual death and moral corruption in the world go side by side. It is the state of spiritual and moral separation from God in this life, which carries on into the next. Warnings of this lost state are found throughout the Bible.

Gen.2:17 ".. 'the day .. you eat of it you shall die'.."
Gen.3:23 ".. God sent him forth from the garden.."
1 Kings 8:46 ".. there is no man who does not sin.."
Ps.14:1 ".. The fool says in his heart, 'There is no God'.."
Jer.17:9 ".. The heart is deceitful .. desperately corrupt.."
Ezk.18:4 ".. the soul that sins shall die.."
Matt.25:46 ".. into eternal punishment.."
Mark 7:21, 23 ".. 'out of the heart of man, come evil thoughts .. they defile a man'.."
Eph.2:2, 3 ".. following the course of this world .. children of wrath.."
1 John 5:12 ".. has not life.."
Rev.2:11 ".. He who conquers shall not be hurt by the second death.."
Rev.21:8 ".. 'fire and brimstone, which is the second death'.."

Christ for our sakes submitted to physical death, and alone conquered it, and rose again triumphant. He left an empty tomb, and His earthly body was never found. Paul longed to meet his Lord. Life is emphasised more in the N.T. than death.

Luke 20:38 ".. but of the living.."
John 20:5 ".. stooping to look in.."
Acts 2:24 ".. God raised him up.."

1 Cor.15:22, 55 " . . in Christ shall all be made alive . . 'O death, where is thy sting?' . . "

2 Cor.5:2 " . . we groan, earnestly desiring . . " (KJV)

Phil.1:21 " . . to die is gain . . "

1 Thes.4:16 " . . the dead in Christ will rise first . . "

Heb.2:14 " . . that through death he might destroy . . death . . "

God is "not God of the dead, but of the living." Jesus on the Cross revealed that the dying can go straight to be with Him in Paradise when He told the dying thief "today you will be with me in paradise". The teaching about "purgatory" has no foundation in Holy Scripture. The power of Satan, sin and death were all met and defeated at the Cross. Therefore spiritual death has no power over the believer in Christ, as John wrote in Revelation:—

Rev.20:6 " . . over such the second death has no power . . "

37: THE PROBLEM OF ADDICTION—alcohol, drugs, gambling

Addiction is a major world problem today. By this (and it can apply to many things other than alcohol) we mean indulgence, demanding "more than enough", craving for, coveting and being a slave of some thing or practice.

Was this the fatal sin into which fell the first two in the Garden of Eden, when they listened to the Devil and took the forbidden fruit when they already had enough of everything? It was a question of obedience, "Yes" or "No" to God's command.

We study the question of **alcohol** as one of the typical things that God had created for man's use, but which has been abused, and to which he easily becomes **addicted**.

Alcohol is the natural product of the action of the spores of yeast on sweet fruit juices in any part of the world. The spores are found attached to the particles of dust in the air and when deposited in any warm sugary fluid develop very rapidly causing fermentation and turning the sugar into alcohol. It is a stimulant, a preservative, and sometimes an anaesthetic, and was used by man from earliest times. The vine was a sign of plenty and a national emblem of the Jewish people. It is mentioned often in the Bible (so also is the sin of drunkenness); its use and abuse, its benefit and its curse are interwoven in the Old Testament.

Gen.9:20, 21 " .. Noah .. became drunk .. "
Gen.9:25 " .. 'Cursed be Canaan' .. " drunkenness brought family trouble.
Deut.7:12, 13 " .. 'God will .. bless .. your grain and your wine and your oil' .. "
Deut.21:20 " .. 'he is a glutton and a drunkard' .. "
Ps.80:8 " .. a vine out of Egypt .. "
Proverbs 23:29, 32 " .. Who has redness of eyes?
Those who tarry long over wine ..
.. it bites like a serpent .. "
Is.5:11 " .. Woe .. run after strong drink .. "
Hab.2:15 " .. Woe to him who makes his neighbours drink .. "
the sin of "treating".

There were **several kinds** of wine in common use (Heb. *yayin*, Gr. *oinos*) mentioned in the Bible, and it was used also as an antiseptic and as an analgesic.

2 Chr.2:10 " .. barrels of wine .. "
Mark 15:23 " .. wine mingled with myrrh .. "
Luke 10:34 " .. pouring on oil and wine .. "
1 Tim.5:23 " .. for the sake of your stomach .. "

Total abstinence was practised from earliest times and was associated with vows and the dedication of one's body to God, such as the life-long vows of the Nazirites, and the priests forbidden to take wine during their term of service in the Temple.

Lev.10:9 " .. Drink no wine .. tent of meeting .. "
Num.6:2 " .. the vow of a Nazirite .. "

Jud.13:4 .. Samson's mother. " .. drink no wine .. "
Dan.1:8 " .. Daniel .. would not defile himself .. "
Luke 1:15 .. John the Baptist. " .. he shall drink no wine .. "

Christ came at a time when religion was dead and bound by endless restrictions and formalism. He had to show the disciples that the Holy Spirit would be their guide in problems of everyday living, in food and drink, in fasting and holy days. The new heart within them was to be their voice of conscience.

Matt.6:16 " .. when you fast .. "
Gal.5:21 " .. drunkenness, carousing .. "
Gal.5:22 " .. the fruit of the Spirit .. self-control .. "
Gal.6:15 " .. for neither .. counts for anything .. but a new creation .. "
John 16:8 " .. 'he will convince the world of sin' .. "

Victory over the craving for alcohol (and other drugs) is promised and the desire may be taken away completely.

1 Cor.10:13 " .. No temptation has overtaken you .. "
1 Cor.10:13 " .. will also provide the way of escape .. "
Jas.4:7 " .. Resist the devil and he will flee .. "

It may be that if Christ had refused to take the ordinary drink of Palestine (which seems to have been a very mild, light wine) His followers would later on have assumed that total abstinence was a necessity for salvation. Some denominations, even as it is, insist on a pledge of total abstinence. This would have tended to nullify, in this one point, the very freedom of grace for which Christ died, and which has become our heritage.

Gal.2:21 " .. if righteousness were through the law, then Christ died to no purpose .. "
Col.2:23 " .. of no value in checking the indulgence of the flesh .. "

In conclusion, modern methods of distilling (making the alcohol content much higher) unknown previously have been largely responsible for the problem of drunkenness that faces the world today. Unquestionably excessive drinking has become one of the curses of mankind. The same can be said of some other drugs such as the wonderful pain-relieving drugs of morphia and cocaine which can become mind-destroying and character-changing when addiction comes in. People can become addicts on other things such as *making money, speculation, gambling* and *drug-taking.*

Every committed Christian has free will to decide prayerfully whether or not his liberty in these things is a risk to himself and also a stumbling block to a weaker brother.

In countries where drunkenness has reached alarming proportions, and is causing untold misery and wickedness, it is doubtful whether this liberty still remains. There are not many true Christians who can take alcohol with an easy conscience.
Christ says:—

Matt.6:24 " .. You cannot serve God and mammon .. "
Matt.18:6 " .. whoever causes .. to sin .. better .. drowned .. "
Luke 21:34 " .. take heed .. drunkenness and cares of this life .. "

And Paul says:—

Rom.13:13 " . . not in revelling and drunkenness . . "

Rom.13:14 " . . make no provision for the flesh, to gratify its desires . . "

Rom.14:13 " . . decide never to put a stumbling block . . in the way of a brother . . "

Rom.14:21 " . . it is right not to . . drink wine . . "

1 Cor.5:11 " . . not to associate with . . greed . . "

1 Cor.6:10 " . . nor drunkards . . will inherit the kingdom of God . . "

1 Cor.8:9 " . . take care lest this liberty of yours somehow become a stumbling block . . "

1 Cor.8:11-13 " . . the brother for whom Christ died . . "

Eph.5:18 " . . And do not get drunk . . "

1 Thes.5:6-8 " . . let us keep awake and be sober . . "

1 Cor.6:19 " . . Do you not know that your body is a temple of the Holy Spirit within you . .
you were bought with a price.
So glorify God in your body."

38: PRIESTHOOD—and Ministry

From the time of the Fall God provided a way of salvation and forgiveness for man. Every individual sinner could approach God through atonement for his sin, by repenting and offering the prescribed sacrifice, in anticipation of the cross of Christ. In all parts of the world anthropologists find evidence of blood sacrifice. In Genesis it is laid down that unhewn stones were to be used for making the altar, and that there were to be no steps leading up to it, so that the humblest man would be able to approach God without hindrance, and at any time. There was no need for a priest. **Every man was his own sacrificing priest**; Heb. *kohen*, Gr. *hiereus*, Lat. *sacerdos*.

Also, it appears, **heads of families** could sacrifice for their households and **patriarchs and kings** such as Melchizedek could sacrifice for their people. The essential requirements of the individual remained unchanged, personal forgiveness through atonement for sin, by sacrifice.

Gen.4:4 " . . and Abel brought of the firstlings of his flock . . "
Gen.8:20 " . . Noah built an altar . . "
Gen.14:18 " . . Melchizedek . . priest of God . . "
Ex.20:25, 26 " . . not build it of hewn stones . . not go up by steps . . "
Josh.8:31 " . . an altar of unhewn stones . . "
Job 1:5 " . . Job would send and sanctify them . . "

Man has always been rebellious and this simple God-given way was soon forsaken in self-will, and other ways and other religions of human effort, typified by Cain's bloodless sacrifice, spread throughout the antediluvian world. Sodom and Gomorrah typified the end-result in Abraham's time.

Then God chose Abraham, to go out in faith from Ur of the Chaldees with all his family, to a land that He would show him and there He would make of him "**a kingdom of priests**". This holy nation, the Jews, would follow His commandments and restore true religion in the world. But the bias towards spiritual degeneration continued.

Ex.19:5 " . . if you will obey . . you shall be my own possession among all peoples . . "
Ex.19:6 " . . a kingdom of priests . . "
Ex.32:4, 25 " . . made a molten calf . . to their shame . . "
Deut.7:6 " . . a people holy to the Lord . . "
Num.25:1 " . . began to play the harlot . . "

God appointed the tribe of Levi to act for the people in their sacrificial worship. But the people denied their unique character by asking for a King, to be like all the nations, and finally they were divided and defeated and driven from their land, although God raised up many of the prophets to call them back to Him. A legalistic remnant who returned failed to recognise "The Lamb of God", their Messiah, and crucified Him.

Ex.28:1 " . . Aaron . . to serve me as priests . . "
Num.8:6 " . . Take the Levites . . "
1 Sam.8:5, 19 " . . But the people refused to listen . . "
2 Chr.36:14 " . . leading priests . . exceedingly unfaithful . . "

Jer.5:31 " . . my people love to have it so . . "
Hos.6:9 " . . so the priests . . murder . . "
Mal.3:7 " . . I will return to you, says the Lord . . "

The age of visible sacrifice came to an end with the destruction of Jerusalem in A.D.70. The consummation of all sacrifice came about when Christ died for the world and shed His blood on the Cross. This opened up "a new and living way", and the dispensation of grace began. The veil of the Holy of Holies was split from top to bottom, and, as at the beginning every man had direct access to God again. Thus there came about the "Priesthood of all Believers", who offer spiritual sacrifices to God of their personal consecration, praise, and thanksgiving.

In the Christian Church there can be no priests in any sense other than this.

Rom.12:1 " . . present your bodies as a living sacrifice . . "
Heb.10:19 " . . confidence to enter the sanctuary . . "
Heb.10:20 " . . through the curtain . . "
Heb.10:22 " . . our hearts sprinkled clean . . "
Heb.13:15 " . . offer up a sacrifice of praise . . "
1 Pet.2:9 " . . a chosen race, a royal priesthood . . "
Rev.1:6 " . . made us a kingdom, priests to his God . . "

What is the difference between "Priesthood" and "Ministry"?
There must be meetings for prayer, praise, preaching and the breaking of bread. This necessitates church officers, but these, of course, are not spiritual intermediaries. Christ is there in the midst, as He said: "Where two or three are gathered together in my name, there am I in the midst of them".

A true Elder (Presbyter, Pastor or Minister, Gr. *presbuteros*) is a man who claims to have had a real call, has been recognised by the local Church, and has been truly filled with the Spirit. Special gifts of the Spirit for administration were promised after Pentecost. This person humbly acts as shepherd, as organiser, and for discipline. He is the minister of the laity, and has the directing of corporate worship, and the administration of the Lord's Supper, and a special commission to tend the flock, but is warned against "lording it over them". The thought of a priest, in the sense of a "sacrificing priest", Lat. "*sacerdos*", having to be present, when the Lord is already there in the midst as He promised, is unbiblical.

Matt.18:20 " . . there am I in the midst . . "
Acts 6:3 " . . pick out . . seven men of good repute . . appoint to this duty . . "
Acts 13:1 " . . Now in the church at Antioch there were prophets and teachers . . "
Acts 14:23 " . . appointed elders . . in every church . . "
Acts 20:17 " . . called to him the elders of the church . . "
1 Cor.14:26–40 . . "When you come together . . decently and in order . . "
1 Tim.3:2 " . . temperate, sensible, dignified, hospitable . . "
1 Tim.5:17 " . . elders who rule well . . "
1 Pet.5:1 " . . so I exhort the elders . . "
1 Pet.5:2 " . . Tend the flock of God . . "

1 Pet.5:3 " . . not as domineering over those in your charge . .
being examples to the flock . . "

The word Priest can have two meanings in English. In the Bible it invariably has the meaning of "sacrificing priest", Heb. "*kohen*", Gr. "*hiereus*". But it is used in the 1662 Book of Common Prayer in several places shortened from the Greek word "presbyteros" = elder, or minister. There is no connection whatever between the O.T. "sacrificing priest" and the N.T. "elder", but the use of the word Priest in the Rubrics before the Absolution and the Ordination Service is unfortunate and misleading.

Apostolic Succession. This is of two kinds—the true, and the false. The true is a life and work like those of the apostles, and in this sense every true soul-winner, whether clerical or lay, is a successor of the apostles. The false rests on an unprovable assumption that there has never been a break in the succession of bishops from the apostles to our own day. Even if this theory were true, the succession would be worthless in the case of any bishop or minister whose spiritual life is out of harmony with the spirit of the apostles. God's grace is not handed down mechanically.

The Lord Jesus—our High Priest.

The only time that the word *hiereus*, sacrificing priest, is used in the N.T. is:—

For the Jewish Priests:

Matt.2:4 " . . all the chief priests . . "

Luke 1:5 " . . a priest named Zechariah . . "

For Christian believers (clergy and laymen) as they offer their spiritual sacrifices:

Heb.13:15 " . . a sacrifice of praise . . "

For the Lord Jesus as our High Priest:

Heb.10:21 " . . having an high priest . . " (KJV)

39: RESURRECTION—Coming back to life

Resurrection means return to life, or rising from the dead. In the theological sense it is used for the foundation truth and doctrine of the coming back of our Lord Jesus Christ from the grave after His crucifixion, which established the fact that He was truly the Son of God, and had power (Rom.1:4). The Bible reveals Him as now seated at the right hand of God. Therefore He is bound up with the believer's own resurrection, and it adds certainty to faith. It also adds assurance of the Lord's Second Coming.

In the Old Testament, although we find no clear statements respecting the resurrection of the dead before the time of the prophets (but see Exodus 3:6, compare Mathew 22, 29 to 32) evidence is not lacking for belief in the resurrection long before the exile. Certainly it was experienced by faith in the individual.

Gen.22:5 with Heb.11:19 " . . to raise men even from the dead . . "
2 Kings 4:32-35 " . . opened his eyes . . "
Job 19:25 " . . for I know that my Redeemer lives . . "
Ps.16:10 " . . thou dost not give me up to Sheol . . "
Is.26:19 " . . Thy dead shall live . . "
Dan.12:2 " . . and many . . shall awake . . "
Hosea 13:14 " . . from the power of Sheol . . "

In the New Testament Christ raised people from the dead, and foretold His own death and resurrection.

Matt.9:25 " . . and the girl arose . . "
Matt.10:8 " . . raise the dead . . "
Matt.12:39 " . . the sign of the prophet Jonah . . "
Matt.16:21 " . . Jesus began to show his disciples . . "
Matt.17:3 " . . there appeared to them Moses and Elijah . . "
Matt.27:52, 53 " . . the saints . . appeared to many . . "
Matt.28:1-7 " . . he has risen . . "
Mark 10:34 " . . after three days he will rise . . "
Luke 7:15 " . . the dead man sat up . . "
John 11:43, 44 " . . Lazarus, come out . . "
John 10:17 " . . I lay down my life . . "
Luke 24:1-8 " . . they remembered his words . . "

The disciples after seeing and communicating with the risen Christ, and having received the promised Holy Spirit, went forth into the world as changed men and women witnessing to the resurrection.

Acts 1:22 " . . a witness to his resurrection . . "
Acts 2:31, 32 " . . he . . spoke of the resurrection . . "
Acts 4:2 " . . proclaiming in Jesus the resurrection . . "
Acts 17:18 " . . because he preached Jesus and the resurrection . . "
Acts 23:8 " . . the Sadducees . . no resurrection . . "
Acts 24:15 " . . both the just and the unjust . . "
1 John 1:1-3 " . . we . . testify to it . . "

Paul frequently refers to the resurrection as the basis of faith and hope.

Acts 13:37 " . . he whom God raised up . . "
Acts 17:31 " . . raising him from the dead . . "

Acts 26:8 " . . Why is it thought incredible . . ?"
Rom.1:4 " . . by his resurrection . . "
Rom.5:10 " . . much more . . by his life . . "
Rom.6:4 " . . Christ was raised from the dead . . "
Rom.14:9 " . . to this end Christ died . . "
1 Cor.15:23 " . . Christ the first fruits . . "
1 Cor.15:51-57 " . . O death, where is thy sting? . . "
Eph.1:20 " . . at his right hand . . "
Phil.3:10 " . . the power of his resurrection . . "
2 Thess.1:10 " . . when he comes on that day . . "
2 Tim.1:10 " . . who abolished death . . "

40: THE AFTER-LIFE—Hell

The dictionaries describe Hell as "The abode of the dead" or "The place and state of condemned spirits"—that is to say, the terminus toward which human life moves. What does the Bible tell us about this after-life?

In the Old Testament the Hebrew word "Sheol" is always used (thirty-one times) for this place and literally means "the underworld", the place of departed spirits, good and bad, a place of sorrow.

Gen.42:38 ".. with sorrow to Sheol.."
Deut.32:22 ".. to the depths of Sheol.."
2 Sam.22:6 ".. the cords of Sheol.."
Ps.88:3 ".. near to Sheol.."
Ps.116:3 ".. the snares of death.."
Jonah 2:2 ".. 'out of the belly of Sheol I cried'.."
Is.14:9–17.. The dead are conscious.
Ezk.32:21.. The dead speak.

Apostasy in Israel brought death and punishment very near. The Valley of Hinnom in N.W. of Jerusalem was used for heathen idol worship and human sacrifices, till it had to be cursed by the prophet Jeremiah.

2 Chr.28:3, 4.. Human sacrifices in Hinnom.
2 Chr.33:6.. Enchantment and witchcraft in Hinnom.
Jer.7:30–34 ".. the valley of.. Hinnom.. shall become a waste.."

So we come to the New Testament—the Greek word *Hades* translates *Sheol* (used 10 times), but a new word appears *Gehenna* (used 21 times)—the latter comes almost entirely from the lips of Christ himself, with *terrible warning*. He refers to *Hades* as being like that cursed valley of Hinnom.

Matt.5:22 ".. danger of hell fire.." Gr. *gehenna* (KJV)
Matt.10:28 ".. soul and body in hell.."
Matt.23:15–33 ".. you.. hypocrites.. child of hell.."
Mark 9:43 ".. unquenchable fire.."
Rev.19:20 ".. the lake of fire.."

Then a new day dawns, Christ reveals Paradise. He says there are two parts of Hades, one for the saved, one for the lost. He uses the beautiful Persian word, *pairidaeza* (the walled garden of kings) for the place of the departed believers, where they are waiting, (a) conscious, (b) comforted, and (c) resting. He says to the dying thief on the cross "today thou shalt be with me in Paradise."

Luke 16:23–26.. Dives in torment, Lazarus comforted.
Luke 23:43 ".. today.. in Paradise.."
1 Cor.15:52 ".. in the twinkling of an eye.."
Acts 2:31.. Christ conquered Hell.
2 Cor.12:1–4.. Paul was allowed to see Paradise.
Eph.4:8–10.. Christ visits Hades: and comes back.
Phil.1:23 ".. to depart and be with Christ.."
Rev.1:18.. Christ has ".. the keys of Death and Hades.."

But Christ's last warning to the world remains.
Luke 13:5 ".. 'unless you repent'.."

41: THE AFTER-LIFE—Heaven

Christ chose the well-known word "Paradise", which the Jews used for the garden of Eden (see LXX), to describe the blissful place where His loved ones would go and where they would be with Him, after death. The Jews believed that all the righteous and chosen departed were in some concealed and hidden place, waiting for the Messiah. Christ drew the veil aside and revealed that place more clearly. It is the very Kingdom of Heaven which He, the Messiah, had come to proclaim and die for, in order that all mankind could enter in.

What does the Bible tell us about heaven? It is

Created by God
> Gen.1:1, 31 " .. In the beginning God created the heavens .. behold, it was very good .. "
> Gen.2:8 " .. the Lord God planted a garden in Eden .. "
> Is.65:17 " .. 'I create new heavens and a new earth' .. " (to be revealed after Christ's second coming)
> Rev.2:7 " .. to him who conquers I will grant to eat .. in the paradise of God .. "

The destiny of all children of God
> Eph.3:15 " .. the whole family in heaven .. " (KJV)

Everlasting
> Ps.89:29 " .. I will establish .. for ever .. as the days of the heavens .. "
> 2 Cor.5:1 " .. we have a building from God .. eternal in the heavens .. "

Immeasurable
> Ps.103:11 " .. the heavens are high above the earth .. "
> Jer.31:37 " .. If the heavens above can be measured .. "
> Is.57:15 " .. the high and lofty One who inhabits eternity .. "

Holy
> Deut.26:15 " .. Look down from thy holy habitation, from heaven .. "
> Ps.20:6 " .. from his holy heaven .. "
> Is.57:15 " .. in the high and holy place .. "

God's dwelling place
> 1 Kings 8:30 " .. in heaven thy dwelling place .. "
> Is.66:1 " .. Heaven is my throne .. "

Christ, the great Mediator, opens the way to heaven
> Heb.6:20 " .. Jesus has gone as a forerunner on our behalf .. "
> Heb.9:12, 24 " .. he entered once for all .. "
> Matt.28:18 " .. All authority in heaven and on earth .. "
> 1 Pet.3:22 " .. at the right hand of God .. "

Angels in heaven
> Matt.18:10 " .. in heaven their angels .. "
> Mark13:32 " .. not even the angels in heaven .. "

Names written in heaven
> Luke10:20 " .. your names are written in heaven .. "
> Heb.12:23 " .. enrolled in heaven .. "

Repentance occasions joy
    Luke 15:7 " . . joy in heaven over one sinner who repents . . "
A place prepared
    John 14:3 " . . I go and prepare a place for you . . "
A place of reward
    Matt.5:12 " . . Rejoice . . your reward is great in heaven . . "
Longing for heaven
    Phil.1:23 " . . with Christ . . far better . . "

42: BAPTISM—Initiation

Much controversy and misunderstanding has grown up around this subject. Let us therefore seek to understand the true meaning. The actual word Gr. *baptizo* means to dip or cleanse in water. The word is used in the New Testament of cleansing things as well as "baptizing" persons. As regards persons, from very early Christian times sprinkling was allowed as well as immersion. It signifies before men, and seals before God, the faith and the cleansing from sin that has taken place in the heart.

> **Mark 7:4** " . . when they come from the market . . they purify ("baptize") themselves . . "

The Origin of Baptism. The idea of ceremonial purification by the use of water was known among the ancient peoples, and the same practice is found in the Old Testament.

The immersion of the whole body, in running water if possible, was a means of washing away ceremonial uncleanness.

The ceremonial washings prescribed by Moses seem to have been considerably added to after the Old Testament period, and by the time of the coming of Christ, baptism or ceremonial cleansing was demanded from all Jewish proselytes equally with circumcision. In this way the Old Testament ceremonial cleansing became the forerunner of Christian baptism.

> **Ex.19:10** " . . Go to the people and consecrate them . . wash their garments . . "
> **Ex.29:4** " . . bring Aaron and his sons . . wash them with water . . "
> **Lev.14:8, 9** " . . bathe himself in water . . bathe his body in water . . "
> **Num.8:7** " . . sprinkle the water of expiation . . "
> **Num.19:13** " . . because the water for impurity was not thrown upon him . . "
> **2 Chr.4:6** " . . ten lavers . . for the priests to wash in . . "
> **2 Kings 5:10** " . . Go and wash in the Jordan . . "
> **Ps.51:2, 7** " . . cleanse me from my sin! . . wash me . . whiter than snow . . "
> **Is.1:16** " . . Wash yourselves; make yourselves clean . . "

The Baptism of John. When John the Baptist came, and by God's command baptized, he was introducing no new custom, but he called upon the backslidden nation to repent and believe in the coming Messiah, and to demonstrate their new repentance and faith before men by stepping into the waters of Jordan, which was to them a sign of the washing away of sin and of their new commitment.

> **Mark 1:4** " . . preaching a baptism of repentance . . "
> **John 1:6** " . . a man sent from God . . "
> **John 1:33** " . . he who sent me to baptize . . "
> **John 1:36** " . . Behold, the Lamb of God . . "
> **John 1:37** " . . two disciples . . followed Jesus . . "
> **Luke 7:30** " . . but the Pharisees and the lawyers rejected the purpose of God . . "

Luke 16:16 " . . men are pressing into it (the kingdom) . . "
(Phillips)
John 4:1 " . . baptizing more disciples than John . . "

The Baptism of Jesus.
Matt.3:13 " . . Jesus came . . to be baptized . . "
Matt.3:15 " . . it is fitting . . to fulfil all righteousness . . "
Matt.3:16 " . . the Spirit of God . . like a dove . . "
Matt.3:17 " . . a voice from heaven . . This is my beloved Son . . "

Christian Baptism. When Christ Himself came He adopted the Jewish practice of baptism and commanded that it should be carried on in a new form by His followers, thereby giving it a deeper and fuller meaning, which was expounded more fully by Paul, after His atoning death had taken place. For the first time it was to be in the name of the Father, the Son and the Holy Spirit. For the Christian, baptism has several aspects:

a. *A public testimony* to accepting Christ as one's personal Saviour and Lord.

b. *A sign of incorporation* in the Visible Church.

c. *A symbolism* that one's sins have been washed away.

Matt.28:19 " . . baptizing them in the name of the Father and of the Son and of the Holy Spirit . . "
Luke 3:16 " . . he will baptize you with the Holy Spirit . . "
John 3:5 " . . born of water and the Spirit . . "
Acts 2:38 " . . Repent, and be baptized . . "
Acts 8:37 " . . See, here is water . . "
Acts 10:47 " . . Can anyone forbid water . . "
Acts 18:25 " . . knew only the baptism of John . . "
Acts 22:16 " . . Rise and be baptized . . "
Rom.6:4 " . . buried . . with him by baptism . . " This passage is spiritual and figurative only.
Eph.4:5 " . . one Lord, one faith, one baptism . . "

In conclusion it is clear that men are saved by:—Faith in the atoning blood of Jesus, accompanied by true repentance, and witnessed to by Baptism, the sign of the Christian covenant.

The Bible is silent on the controversial question of how much water is to be used in the rite, whether by affusion (sprinkling) or immersion (completely immersed): books have been written convincingly on both sides. One must conclude that the amount of water used is not of vital import; if it were so God would have specified clearly.

By whom is the ceremony of Baptism carried out?

Naturally this will be done by the minister before all the assembly of Christians, but as stated above there is once again no clear directive in the Bible as to who this should be. We must beware of the sacerdotal error that the person, or infant, is born again by the actual performance of the ceremony—*ex opere operato*, i.e. "by the act performed".

Apparently Christ Himself never baptized, and Paul very rarely.
John 4:2 " . . although Jesus himself did not baptize . . "
1 Cor.1:14 " . . I am thankful that I baptized none of you except . . "

Is Baptism essential?

There are some who understand the teaching of our Lord and of Paul differently and who hold that no ceremonial act of baptism is necessary. We can well believe that people are saved by repentance and faith without the sign. There are circumstances where baptism is impossible or impracticable such as the dying thief on the cross. In no case can the sign effect anything apart from personal faith in Christ.

Luke 23:43 " . . today you will be with me in Paradise . . "
Jer.2:22 " . . 'Though you wash . . your guilt is still before me' . . "
Rom.10:10 " . . believes with his heart . . and confesses with his
    lips . . "
Gal.6:15 " . . but a new creation . . "

Infant Baptism.

It is doubtful if we can get direct evidence from the Bible one way or the other, as regards Infant Baptism. Perhaps Acts 2:38, 39; 16:15, 33 are the nearest. The Protestant Churches which practise it believe that as our Lord commanded the little children to be brought to Him, so He wills that the children of His own people should be dedicated to Him from the first. And they believe that the best way of doing this is by the sign of baptism. Infants are baptized on the charitable assumption that they will claim for themselves one day by personal faith in Christ, the new birth of which their baptism was the sign. It is not only in Infant Baptism that the sign comes first and the faith comes afterwards.

But it is impossible for any man to be born again except by personal faith in Christ. The case of those who die as infants or very young children is special. They rest in the love of God which they have never rejected.

43: THE LORD'S SUPPER—Holy Communion

This observance is also spoken of as the **Breaking of Bread, the Lord's Supper**, or the **Eucharist** (Gr. *eucharistia*, "thankfulness"). The simplest form of worship was first carried out in the simplest of buildings—the home. It was originally the "*agape*" or "fellowship meal", a "love feast", for those who loved the Lord; but to the shame of His followers it has become the battleground of controversy. Christendom is divided over this sacred service, therefore it is important to understand clearly its origin, and meaning.

It originated in the changing by Christ of the Jewish evening Passover feast, into a Christian supper of remembrance. He Himself "The Lamb" about to be slain took the unleavened bread of the Passover, and the wine drunk at the Passover Meal, and made them the symbols of His Body, about to be broken and His Blood about to be shed. He thus fulfilled and brought to an end this special Old Testament ceremony which was a picture in shadow of which He had become the reality. Thus the Passover became the Lord's Supper, as it is called by Paul:

1 Cor.11:20–34 " . . the Lord's supper . . "
1 Cor.11:24 " . . Do this in remembrance of me . . "

The Old Testament background. The Passover was held in the second week of the Jewish New Year. It was a time of re-dedication and of family reunion and rejoicing. It was a time of looking back to what God had done for them, a remembering of their salvation out of Egypt. It was a solemn duty and privilege to attend. The symbolical meaning was passed on from father to son.

Ex.12:11 " . . It is the Lord's passover . . "
Ex.13:8 " . . you shall tell your son on that day . . "
Deut.16:1 " . . Observe the month of Abib . . "
Joshua 5:10 " . . they kept the passover . . "
1 Sam.20:6 " . . there is a yearly sacrifice there . . "
2 Chr.30:15 " . . And they killed the passover lamb . . "
Is.30:29 " . . a song as in the night . . "
Ezk.45:10–21 . . Repentance, the Passover, and revival comes.

The origin of the Lord's Supper. Undoubtedly the original Passover was intended to be a picture of Christ's sacrifice for us. He Himself took the place (on the Cross) of the slain lamb. He was "The Lamb slain from the foundation of the world." As He died, He cried, "It is finished." His death was the end of the old era, and just before it took place, in one of the last commands He gave to His disciples, He instituted a new Christian memorial, linked with the former Passover.

1 Cor.5:7 " . . Christ our paschal lamb . . "
1 Pet.1:19 " . . with the precious blood of Christ . . "
Rev.5:6 " . . I saw a Lamb standing . . "
Rev.13:8 " . . the Lamb slain from the foundation of the world . . "
(KJV)
John 1:29 " . . Behold, the Lamb of God . . "
Luke 22:7 " . . Then came the day of . . the passover . . "
Luke 22:15 " . . I have earnestly desired to eat this passover . . "

Luke 22:19a " . . This is my body . . " (N.B. There is no "*is*" in Aramaic).
Luke 22:19b " . . this do in remembrance of me . . " (KJV)

The meaning of the Lord's Supper. What is meant by feeding spiritually on the body and blood of Christ? In our Lord's discourse on the Bread of Life in John, chapter 6, He says much about feeding on His flesh and blood. Verse 53 sums up the teaching: "Except ye eat the flesh of the Son of Man, and drink his blood, ye have no life in you." These words were said before the Lord's Supper was instituted, and so cannot be limited to it: they refer to a spiritual act, of which the Lord's Supper is the sacramental sign.

John 6:48-58 " . . How can this man give us his flesh to eat? . . "

What then is that spiritual act? To feed on the body of Christ broken for us, and His blood shed for us, is to take to ourselves afresh in grateful faith and remembrance what He did on the cross, as done for us (even as in literal eating we make our own, the food which we take into our bodies). It is to claim personal forgiveness through the cross and to rejoice in it, and to enter into closer union with our Lord. Such spiritual feeding on Christ is not possible if the heart is cherishing anything out of harmony with Him. On the other hand, being an act of the heart not of the body, it can be done at any place and at any time, but especially at this memorial supper.

John 6:56 " . . He who eats my flesh . . abides in me . . "

Christ often used picture language. Christ often represented Himsel to His disciples in picture language, such as: the Vine, the Good Shepherd, the Water of Life. Likewise at the institution of the new Christian Supper of Remembrance, He says that the bread and the wine were always to be the sacred symbols of His broken body and of His blood poured out. The outward actions of eating the bread and drinking the wine are pictures of the inward action of feeding on what the bread and wine represent. Thus in the Book of Common Prayer it is said: "Take and eat this" (the outward act) "in remembrance that Christ died for thee, and feed on Him in thy heart by faith with thanksgiving" (the inward act). Those who say that the Body of Christ is somehow *in* the bread ruin the whole meaning of the sacrament, because it is the heart, not the mouth, that must feed upon Him. The outward act of eating with the mouth is worthless apart from the inward act of feeding on Christ with the heart.

Matt.26:26 " . . Take, eat; this is my body . . "
Matt.26:28 " . . this is my blood . . "
John 4:14 " . . the water that I shall give . . "
John 10:11 " . . I am the good shepherd . . "
John 15:1, 4 " . . I am the true vine . . Abide in me . . "

It is clear then that partaking of the Lord's Supper is of no avail for one who has not yet received Christ by faith, and who is still dead in sin. You cannot feed a dead body—but furthermore, if a Christian goes to Communion with cherished sin and unsurrendered wrongs in his heart he is deliberately refusing the cleansing of the blood of Christ and as Paul says to the Corinthian converts:—

I Cor.11:29 " . . For anyone who eats and drinks without discerning the body eats and drinks judgment upon himself. That is why many of you are weak and ill, and some have died . . "

The Doctrine of the "Real Presence". The teaching of the changing of the whole substance of the eucharistic bread and wine into the body and blood respectively of Christ is held in the Doctrine of the Mass, but was rejected by the Reformers.

It has been truly said, "Christ is at the table and not on it ."

The administration of Holy Communion. The term Breaking of Bread (the earliest name of the Lord's Supper) suggests an informal gathering rather than a church service as we now understand it. The New Testament gives no formal rules as to who should preside, or as to the place, or the time of meeting. During the first century it appears to have been the custom to administer the bread and wine at the close of a common evening meal. It became the custom after the second century for elders to preside as a necessity of church order.

John 20:19 " . . the first day of the week . . Jesus came . . "
Acts 2:46 " . . breaking bread in their homes . . "
Acts 20:7 " . . On the first day of the week . . to break bread . . "

The return of our Lord.

There is a beautiful Jewish custom in connection with the Passover Supper: an empty chair is placed at the head of the table, because it is believed that the Messiah will one day return on a Passover night.

44: THE BIBLE—Inspiration

This term when applied to the Bible affirms that "the various writers, all down the ages, were impelled to write, and controlled in thought and vocabulary by the Holy Spirit. The literature produced by them was therefore free from error, and in a unique and vital sense the Word of God. This does not imply any mechanical dictation, or loss of personality in the writer, but they were guided in such a way that false history and inaccurate description were avoided" (T. C. Hammond). "Inspired," represents the Greek *theopneustos* = "God-breathed". It is as difficult to define exactly *how* the Scriptures were inspired as it is to explain *how* our Lord was conceived by the Holy Spirit. But if we believe in His full Divinity it is as logical to believe in the full inspiration of *His* written Word.

The Bible claims clearly to be God's Word to man. Continually we read the words "Thus saith the Lord" or "the Word of the Lord came".

Ex.24:4 " . . wrote all the words of the Lord . . "
Ex.32:16 " . . the writing of God . . "
Deut.31:24 . . The Scrolls kept in the ark.
Is.1:2 . . The vision of Isaiah.
Is.28:16 " . . says the Lord . . "
Jer.5:14 " . . Therefore thus says the Lord . . "
Ezk.2:7 " . . speak my words . . "
Ezk.3:3 " . . sweet as honey . . "
Zech.7:7 " . . by the former prophets ? . . "
1 Thes.2:13 " . . it really is, the word of God . . "
2 Tim.3:16 " . . All scripture is inspired by God . . "
2 Peter 1:20, 21 " . . moved by the Holy Spirit . . "

The following testify to certain occasions when a direct command from God to write was given, and St Paul intimates very clearly that his message both spoken and written came direct from God.

Moses—
Ex.17:14 " . . Write this . . "
Isaiah—
Is.8:1 " . . write upon it . . "
Is.30:8 " . . on a tablet . . "
Jeremiah—
Jer.30:2 " . . Write in a book . . "
Jer.36:2 " . . Take a scroll . . "
Habakkuk—
Hab.2:2 " . . Write the vision . . "
John—
Rev.1:19 " . . write what you see . . "
Rev.21:5 " . . Write this . . trustworthy and true . . "
Paul—
Rom.16:26 " . . made known to all nations . . "
1 Cor.11:23 " . . from the Lord . . "

Gal.1:11 " . . not man's gospel . . "
Eph.3:4 " . . the mystery . . "
1 Thes.2:13 " . . not . . word of men . . "
1 Thes.4:15 " . . the coming of the Lord . . "
1 Tim.4:1 " . . the Spirit expressly says . . "

Christ vindicates the Divine authorship of the Old Testament and promised a further revelation by the Holy Spirit after His death, and He also claimed the full authority of His Father for all His own utterances.

Matt.4:4 " . . It is written . . "
Matt.19:4 " . . Have you not read . . "
Matt.26:54 " . . be fulfilled . . "
Luke 4:21 " . . Today . . been fulfilled . . "
Luke 24:27 " . . he interpreted . . the scriptures . . "
Luke 24:45 " . . he opened their minds . . "
John 5:46 " . . he . . " (Moses) " . . wrote of me . . "
John 17:8 " . . I have given them the words which thou gavest
    me . . "

The Bible speaks with authority, and convicts. It is "the sword of the Spirit". The human and Divine elements of Scripture are as incapable of separation as is the Divine and human nature of Our Lord. The Bible is capable of revealing the meaning intended by God in every age and in every circumstance in which a man may find himself, provided he is willing to be taught by the Holy Spirit. God has commanded that the Bible be read and taught. Renewed study of the Bible can lead to Revival.

Jos.1:8 " . . meditate on it day and night . . "
2 Kings 23:2 (and 2 Chr.34:15) " . . the king . . read . . " and
    Revival came.
Ez.10:1 " . . confession, weeping . . "
Neh.8:1 " . . the people gathered . . before the Water Gate . . "
Ps.1:2 " . . his delight . . "
Ps.119:105 " . . a lamp to my feet . . "
Acts 17:11 " . . examining the scriptures daily . . "
Rom.15:4 " . . written for our instruction . . "
Eph.6:17 " . . the sword of the Spirit . . "
1 Thes.5:27 " . . this letter be read . . "
1 Tim.4:13 " . . public reading . . "
James 1:22 . . A Warning—" . . be doers . . not hearers only . . "

There is a solemn warning to those who *add to* or *take away from* the words of the Bible.

Deut.4:2 " . . not add . . nor take from . . "
Rev.22:18, 19 " . . I warn every one . . "

"Moved by the Holy Spirit" (2 Pet.1:21). Gr. *pheromenoi* means "borne along" by the Spirit like a ship borne along by the wind.

"It should be borne in mind that on no subject has the Church been more united, as on the question of the authenticity of the Scriptures, till the nineteenth century."

By the use of the term "*Ultimate Authority*" is meant that the Bible, as being the Word of God, is the final *Court of Appeal* for committed Christian believers as opposed to "Man's Reason" for humanists and "The Church" for sacerdotalists.

The following points must be remembered when studying the question of the inspiration of the Bible.

(a) It is the *original writings* not the translations that were inspired.

(b) There are inevitably copyists' errors.

(c) Everything recorded in the Bible is not necessarily God's direct message, but the record itself is inspired. For instance, the Scribes said of Jesus, "He hath a devil and is mad"; this was not the truth, but the record is inspired.

(d) The writers of the various books retained their human individuality, but it never affected the truth.

45: THE CHURCH—Invisible and Visible

The old English word "church", or "kirk", may be traced to the Greek *kuriakon*—the Lord's (house). This may be used to refer to a *building*, a *particular body* of Christians, the *whole body* of baptized professing Christians, or the inner circle of *true believers*, alive or departed in the faith of Christ.
The Greek and Latin term, translated as "church" is *ecclesia*, an assembly of "called out" ones. So the true church consists of all those who since the time of Pentecost have been born again and have come out of the bondage of Satan, and become followers of Christ.

The Invisible Church is the true church, composed of those whose names have been written in "the Lamb's Book of Life", known only to God. They are the "hidden remant", the "inner circle", the "true Fellowship" of all Christian congregations and gatherings. They are an organism rather than an organisation. They are all "true believers", past, present and future.

Is.1:9 " . . a very small remnant . . " (KJV)
Matt.13:49 " . . separate the evil from the righteous . . "
John 17:20 " . . for those who believe in me . . "
Acts 2:38 " . . Repent, and be baptized . . "
Rom.11:2-5 " . . who have not bowed the knee . . "
Eph.1:22, 23 " . . the church, which is his body . . "
Eph.2:19 " . . members of the household of God . . "
Eph.5:25 " . . as Christ loved the church . . "—The True Church
2 Tim.2:19 " . . The Lord knows those who are his . . "
1 Peter 2:9 " . . God's own people . . "
1 John 2:19 " . . they were not of us . . "
Rev.7:14 " . . they have washed their robes . . "
Phil.4:3 with Rev.20:15 " . . whose names are in the book of life . . "

The Visible Church is seen in the organised congregations of professed believers in Christ, who meet for prayer, praise and worship. Whenever even two or three are gathered together for fellowship in the name of Christ you have a visible church. The visible church must not be confused with the true church. The former entails membership cards and being written down on baptismal registers. Paul said "all things should be done decently and in order" (1 Cor.14:40) and leaders were chosen and appointed who were called **Elders,** *presbuteroi* taken from the Jewish religious organisation, and **Bishops,** *episcopoi*, and **Deacons,** *diakonoi*, taken from the Greek civil organisation.
In the visible church there will always be unbelievers, the "mixed multitude" ("the tares") till Christ returns. Largely for this reason, true unity is always difficult. Uniformity of external forms of worship must not be confused with unity. Even holding office in this visible church does not in itself guarantee a spiritual relationship with Christ.
In the world there are hundreds, even thousands of sects and denominations calling themselves Christian, but in God's sight there is only one body of true believers.

Ex.12:38 " . . A mixed multitude also went up . . "
Matt.13:24–30 . . The parable of the wheat and the tares (or weeds).
Matt.18:20 " . . where two or three are gathered . . "
Acts 2:42 " . . teaching, and fellowship . . to the breaking of bread and the prayers . . "
Acts 13:2 " . . Set apart for me Barnabas and Saul . . "
Acts 20:7 " . . when we were gathered together . . "
Rom.16:5 " . . greet also the church in their house . . "
1 Cor.1:2 " . . To the church . . at Corinth . . "
1 Cor.14:26 " . . Let all things be done for edification . . "
1 Cor.16:19 " . . The churches of Asia send greetings . . "
Gal.1:22 " . . the churches of Christ in Judea . . "—The Local Congregations.
1 Tim.3:15 " . . the church of the living God . . "
Rev.1:20 " . . the seven churches . . "

The Bible uses several comparisons to illustrate the true Church of God, His "called out" ones in the world.

—It is likened to a **chaste virgin, betrothed to Christ,** who expects in return to Him, faithfulness, purity and absolute love and devotion.
2 Cor.11:2 " . . I betrothed you to Christ . . "
Rev.19:7 " . . the marriage of the Lamb . . "

—It is likened to **the Israelites coming out of Egypt,** a chosen nation, under the blood, and the cloud, and the fire.
Ex.19:6 " . . a holy nation . . "
Deut.10:15 " . . the Lord set his heart in love . . "
Acts 7:38 " . . in the congregation in the wilderness . . "
1 Pet.2:9 " . . a chosen race . . a holy nation . . "

—It is likened to a **holy temple, composed of stones** of diverse colour, shape, and function, in which Christ dwells.
1 Cor.3:16 " . . you are God's temple . . "
Eph.2:20–22 " . . Jesus Himself being the corner stone . . "
1 Pet.2:5 " . . and like living stones . . "

—It is likened to a **human body, with its diverse functions.**
1 Cor.12:12–27 " . . as the body is one and has many members . . "
" . . you are the body of Christ . . "
Eph.5:29 " . . but nourishes and cherishes it, as Christ does the Church . . "

—It is likened to **the bride in a true love-marriage,** where Christ Himself is the husband.
Eph.5:32 " . . This is a great mystery, and I take it to mean Christ and the church . . "
Rev.21:2 " . . as a bride adorned for her husband . . "

Lastly, we must end with **Christ's own message to the Churches** in Asia Minor in the Book of Revelation, which was also obviously prophetic. He warns the Churches of the danger of losing their "first love" and of growing cold and "luke warm". If unrepentant, we lose our testimony, and our light will go out; but all down church history, with undying love, Christ stands at the door and knocks.

    Rev.1:13 " . . in the midst of the lampstands one like a son of man . . "

    Rev.1:20 " . . the seven lampstands are the seven churches . . "

    Rev.2:4 " . . thou hast left thy **first love** . . " (KJV)

    Rev.2:5 " . . remember then from what you have fallen, repent . . "

46: CALL TO MISSION—"Here am I, send me"

The call to Mission is the logical outcome of the changed life. We are changed into His image who said: "As the Father has sent me, even so I send you." It is the outcome of true spiritual vision that sees a lost world as Christ saw it, and is willing to follow in His footsteps. The field is the world, i.e. the place where you were when you were crucified with Him, and "beginning at Jerusalem," i.e. where you were when you were converted. The opportunity of going to foreign lands is only possible for the few, although the call to active mission service is binding on all Christians, on those who remain as much as on those who go.

The Bible explains the true call. There is a vast "cloud of witnesses", "of whom the world was not worthy," who have lived this life. It is the new nature that takes possession of a man, the nature of the Lord Jesus. The called ones are those who have heard God saying, "Who will go?" and have answered, "Here am I, send me," i.e. send me anywhere you like.

> Ex.2:11 " . . and looked on their burdens . . "
> Ex.4:12 " . . I will be with your mouth . . "
> Prov.29:18 " . . Where there is no vision, the people perish . . " (KJV)
> Is.6:1 " . . I saw the Lord . . "
> Is.6:5 " . . Woe is me! . . "
> Is.6:8 " . . Here am I! Send me . . "
> Jer.1:6 " . . Do not say, 'I am only a youth' . . "
> Amos 7:14 " . . I am no prophet . . "
> Matt.9:9 " . . Matthew . . at the tax offiice . . Follow me . . "
> Mark 1:17 " . . Come . . I will make you to become fishers of men . . " (KJV)
> Luke 4:18 " . . to preach good news to the poor . . "
> Luke 24:45–48 " . . You are witnesses . . "
> John 20:21 " . . As the Father has sent me, even so I send you . . "
> Heb.12:1 " . . cloud of witnesses . . "

The Cost of the True Call

> Ex.32:32 " . . if thou wilt forgive their sin . . and if not blot me . . out of thy book . . " Moses willing to be blotted out of the Book of Life, for his brethren.
> Rom.9:3 " . . For I could wish that I myself were accursed . . for the sake of my brethren . . " Paul willing to be accursed for his kinsmen.
> Phil.2:5, 7 " . . Christ Jesus . . emptied himself, taking the form of a servant . . "
> John 3:16 " . . God so loved the world that he gave his Only Son, that whoever believes in him, should not Perish but have Eternal Life . . "

Devotional Study

In seeking guidance about mission we must beware of the false calls. They may ensnare people into the foreign mission-field who are not really meant to go. "It may be harder to face God with your motive, than the audience with your message" (Oswald Chambers).

(a) **The "Humanitarian" Call**
Human need is made the call. We are called to evangelise not to civilise. If educational, industrial or medical work have been allowed to constitute the call, or have the first place, we will be missing the true call of Christ.

(b) **The "Adventure" Call**
"Going to see the world"—"keen on pioneering"—the heroic call! Peter leaped overboard, but later the waves nearly overcame him. (Matt.14:28–31.)

(c) **The "Imitation" Call**
"It's the 'done thing' to be a Missionary"—"All the keen people of the Christian Union become Missionaries." But remember the saying that the devil may "send a man to the foreign mission-field to *stop* him being a true missionary in the place where God wanted him to be!"

(d) **The "Self-Denial" Call**
Devoted lives, relying on works for salvation, driven to bury themselves in self-denying work, determined to give up and to sacrifice all, letting reliance on works take the place of grace. Loneliness may drive a person into this class.

(e) **The "Self-seeking" Call**
In this group are those who say " . . grant us to sit one at your right hand and one at your left . . ", i.e. those who seek earthly promotion, and find it quicker in the mission field. It must be *He* not *I*, if our motive is pure (Mark 10:37).

Gal.2:20 " . . no longer I, but Christ . . "

47: THE SECOND ADVENT—The Second Coming of Christ

The Advent of Christ (by this we mean, the visible coming again of Our Lord Jesus Christ to the world) is foretold in the Bible in a considerable number of passages (1,527 in the O.T. and 319 in the N.T., it is said). After the Birth, Death and Resurrection of the Saviour, there is scarcely anything more important than the **Second Advent**. But as this chapter deals with prophecy and with the future, a subject that has caused much controversy and sometimes sad mistakes, we must pray for the help of the Holy Spirit, and for humility in our study.

The word **Eschatology** is derived from the Greek word *eschatos*, and means "the study of the last things." The **Apocalypse**, Gr. *apokalupsis*—means the "appearing" or "unveiling". Another word used is the Gr. *epiphaneia*, meaning "brightness" or "visibility", hence our word **Epiphany**. Finally, the Gr. word *parousia*, "presence" or "arrival", often used to describe the visits of kings and rulers, is also employed.

1. THE FIRST AND SECOND ADVENTS—O.T. and N.T.

The O.T. clearly predicted the details of Christ's first coming, even describing His death by crucifixion. In view of this we should consider very carefully the repeated prophecies about His second coming. All the Greek words used, including "*parousia*", imply visibility—it is to be a *visible return*. There are two schools of thought about His second coming—The *Historicist*, those who believe that Christ has come back, at Pentecost, conversion, or at death and such like; and the *Futurist*, the viewpoint of this study, that the greatest events of prophecy still lie ahead.

> Ps.22:1-31 " . . My God, my God . . " (written 1,000 years before the Crucifixion).
> Is.53:9a " . . made his grave with the wicked . . "
> Is.53:9b " . . with a rich man in his death . . "
> Dan.7:14 " . . an everlasting dominion . . "—The **reigning** Messiah.
> Micah 5:2 " . . O Bethlehem . . from you shall come . . "
> Zech.11:12, 13 " . . thirty pieces of silver . . " (KJV)
> Zech.12:10 " . . they look on him whom they have pierced . . "
> The **suffering** Messiah.
> Matt.24:30 " . . the sign of the Son of man . . "
> Matt.25:31 " . . When the Son of man comes in his glory . . "
> Luke 24:44 " . . that everything written about me . . "
> John 14:3 " . . I will come again . . "
> Acts 1:3 " . . speaking of the kingdom . . "
> Acts 1:11 " . . Jesus . . will come in the same way . . "
> Acts 13:27 " . . because they did not recognise him nor understand . . the prophets . . "
> 1 Thes.3:13 " . . at the coming of our Lord Jesus . . "
> Titus 2:13 " . . the glorious appearing of . . " (KJV)
> Heb.9:28 " . . Christ . . will appear a second time . . "

Rev.1:3 . . There is a special blessing attached to the reading of the Book of Revelation.

2. BEFORE HE COMES
Before Christ's return certain events must have taken place in the world

a. The Gospel must have been preached throughout the whole world
Matt.24:14a " . . throughout the whole world . . "
Matt.24:14b " . . then the end will come . . "
The Bible has been translated into more than 1,500 main languages of the world. The American and British United Bible Societies sold nearly 6 million Bibles in 1973. The printed page and the mass media of radio and television have reached millions of homes, large and small, urban and rural, around the world. It is said that in America, on the various radio channels, it is possible to tune in to the Gospel at any hour of the day. Can we not say that the Gospel has reached to "the whole world"?

b. A long time, but relatively short in God's reckoning, was to elapse before the end
Matt.24:48 " . . My master is delayed . . "—The parable of the wicked servant.
Mat.25:5 " . . as the bridegroom was delayed . . "—The parable of the ten maidens.
Mat.25:19 " . . Now after a long time . . "—The parable of the talents.

c. The Jews will be preserved as a nation
It is a miracle that Israel still exists after years of dispersion and presecution. But God in His sovereign will has chosen them for the redemption of the world. Israel became an independent nation on May 14th, 1948 after 2,600 years of dispersion. For centuries pious Jews have repeated in the Passover Service: "next year at Jerusalem"—until the Six-Day War, June, 1967, when they took the city.
Deut.30:3 " . . he will gather you again . . "
Is.60:9 " , , the ships of Tarshish first, to bring your sons from far . . "
Jer.30:18 " . . I will restore the fortunes of . . Jacob . . "
Ezk.36:24 " . . and bring you into your own land . . "
Ezk.37:3 " . . can these bones live? . . "
Matt.24:34 " . . this generation will not pass away . . " (Gr. *genea*, race or generation).
Rom.11:25 " . . until the full number . . "

d. There will be many false prophets, perversive ideologies and false Christs
The last hundred years have seen an enormous increase in heretical movements and sects—Christian Science, humanism, militant atheism, scientology, theosophy, modern permissiveness and pornography, spiritism, satanism and the occult, and lately neo-rationalist theology (human reason as the measure of all things, not the Bible) and lastly the new "art", in sculpture, painting, music and architecture.

Matt.24:5 " . . For many will come in my name . . "
Matt.24:11 " . . many false prophets . . lead many astray . . "
Matt.24:24 " . . even the elect . . "
1 Tim.4:1 " . . in later times some will depart . . "
2 Peter 2:1 " . . secretly bring in destructive heresies . . "

e. **"The times of the Gentiles" must have come to an end**
The "times of the Gentiles" began with the captivity of Judah under Nebuchadnezzar in 610 B.C. Since that time Jerusalem had been under Gentile overlordship, until finally it was freed in June, 1967, and the "times of the Gentiles" came to an end.

2 Chron.36:6 " . . Nebuchadnezzar . . bound him in fetters . . "
Luke 21:24 " . . 'Jerusalem will be trodden down . . until the times of the Gentiles are fulfilled' . . "—a near and far prophecy.

3. AT THE TIME OF HIS COMING
At the time of the end certain things will be happening and taking place in the world. We ask, like the disciples, " . . when will this be, and what will be the sign of your coming and of the close of the age?" (Matt.24:3.) In 1908 when Dr. Herzl launched the Zionist movement there were only 41,000 Jews in Palestine. Since that time they have been pouring back into their ancient country and became a nation on May 14th, 1948, and now number several million.

a. **There will have been a return of the Jews** on a large scale to their land
Is.11:11, 12 " . . the Lord will extend his hand . . to recover the remnant . . "
Ezk.37:21–24 " . . ' I will take the people of Israel . . and bring them to their own land' . . "

b. **Unprecedented global distress**, famines, suffering, brain-washing, wars, religious persecution, loss of freedom, pollution and crises. 10 million died in World War I, 1914–18, and 78 million are said to have perished in World War II of 1939–45. It is now said that there are enough stock-piled atomic bombs to destroy mankind. All this leads up to the **Great Tribulation.**

Jer.30:5 " . . a cry of panic . . "
Dan.12:1 " . . a time of trouble, such as never has been . . "
Joel 2:31 " . . before the great and terrible day . . "
Zeph.1:14–16 " . . distress . . ruin . . darkness . . "
Matt.24:9 " . . Then they will deliver you up . . "
Matt.24:10 " . . many will fall away . . betray . . hate . . "
Matt.24:21 " . . there will be great tribulation . . "
Luke 21:11 " . . there will be great earthquakes . . famines . . "
2 Tim.3:1–5 " . . lovers of self, lovers of money, proud . . inhuman . . haters of good . . "

c. **Organised Christianity will be prejudiced and unprepared,** as the Jews were at the time of Christ's first coming. Faith will be wavering and love will have grown cold.

Matt.24:4 " . . Take heed that no one leads you astray . . "
Matt.24:32 " . . From the fig tree learn its lesson . . its leaves . . "

Matt.24:44 " . . the Son of Man is coming at an hour you do not expect . . "

Mark 13:36 " . . and find you asleep . . "

Luke 17:26 " . . As it was in the days of Noah, so will it be . . "

Luke 18:8 " . . will he find faith on earth ? . . "

Luke 21:26 " . . men fainting with fear . . "

Luke 21:34 " . . lest . . that day come upon you suddenly . . "

2 Pet.3:3 " . . scoffers will come in the last days . . "

2 Pet.3:4 " . . saying, Where is the promise of his coming? . . "

d. **Some Christians all over the world will be expecting His return.** They will be ready and waiting, as John the Baptist and a few were for His first coming.

Dan.12:10 " . . those who are wise shall understand . . "

Matt.24:22 " . . for the sake of the elect . . "

Matt.24:46 " . . Blessed is that servant . . find so doing . . "

Matt.25:2 " . . Five of them were foolish, and five were wise . . "

Luke 2:25, 38 . . Simeon and Anna were looking for the Messiah.

Luke 21:36 " . . But watch at all times . . "

Titus 2:13 " . . awaiting our blessed hope, the appearing . . "

e. **Believers who are living at the return of Christ** will be transformed without passing through death. This "rapture" or being "caught up (Lat. *rapere*, to snatch or catch up) to meet the Lord in the air" is Paul's way of describing the experience of transition. (See NBD, p.388.)

Luke 12:37 " . . Blessed are those servants . . awake when he comes . . "

1 Cor.15:51 " . . Lo! I tell you a mystery. We shall not all sleep, but we shall all be changed . . " (Gr. *atomos*, which can mean to become invisible)

1 Thes.4:15–17 " . . we who are alive . . shall be caught up . . to meet the Lord in the air . . "

f. **Satan's age-long opposition to Christ** and His Kingdom seems to be climaxed in the appearance of a world personage called *"The Antichrist"*, also called "The Man of Sin", "The Beast", "The Lawless One". Satan tries to embody in this world ruler what he failed to do in the temptation of Christ.

Dan.7:8 " . . among them another little horn . . " (KJV)

Dan.11:36–45 " . . speak astonishing things . . "

Luke 4:6, 7 " . . worship me, it shall all be yours . . "

2 Thes.2:3 " . . the man of lawlessness is revealed . . "

2 Thes.2:4, 9 " . . by the activity of Satan . . signs and wonders . . "

1 John 2:18 " . . the last hour . . antichrist is coming . . "

Rev.13:4 " . . who is like the beast? . . "

Rev.19:19, 20 " . . thrown alive into the lake of fire . . "

g. **The Bible names the place of this final conflict** between Good and Evil, God and Satan. It is the Plain of Esdraelon, that runs from the Port of Haifa on the coast to the river Jordan, "called in the Hebrew tongue *Armageddon.*" "An enemy from the north"!—the Jews will cry to God.

Ezk.38:8–12, 15, 21, 22 " . . many nations upon the mountains of Israel . . "

Joel 3:1–14 " . . Multitudes, multitudes in the valley of decision! . . "

Zech.12:1–3 " . . in the siege against Jerusalem . . "

Zech 13:9 " . . 'They will call on my name' . . "

Zech.14:4–11 " . . the Mount of Olives shall be split . . "

Rev.16:14–16 " . . called in Hebrew Armageddon . . "

Rom.11:26, 27 " . . all Israel will be saved . . "

4. THE ACTUAL COMING OF THE LORD

This is thought by many Bible students to have two aspects or stages.

It will be as a thief in the night, i.e. suddenly and unexpectedly when the Lord comes for His people to take them up to Himself in the air; the other, when He brings His people with Him to the earth, in His power and great glory. *The first called "the rapture"*, appears to precede the final second coming, at the time of the battle of Armageddon. A new age will be ushered in, the thousand years, or "the millennium". The purpose of the second coming is the glorification of the Lord Jesus Christ and of the True Church—His Bride—called out of "all nations, peoples, kindreds, and tongues," at last triumphant. There will apparently be a final cessation of the present world system, when "the new heaven and new earth" begin.

Zech.14:4 " . . his feet . . on the Mount of Olives . . "

Matt.24:29–31 " . . 'they will see the Son of man coming' . . "

Matt.25:31 " . . all the angels with him . . "

Luke 17:24 " . . For as the lightning flashes . . "

Luke 21:27 " . . in a cloud with power and great glory . . "

Acts 1:11 " . . in the same way as you saw him go . . "

(Gr. —*in exactly the same manner*)

Col.3:4 " . . you also will appear with him . . "

1 John 2:28 " . . not shrink . . in shame at his coming . . "

The final judgment of sin

Matt.13:39 " . . the harvest is the close of the age . . "

2 Cor.5:10 " . . all appear before the judgement seat of Christ . . "

Heb.9:27 " . . after that comes judgement . . "

2 Peter 3:13b " . . in which righteousness dwells . . "

Rev.1:7 " . . all the tribes of the earth will mourn . . " (NASB)

Rev.20–12 " . . the dead were judged . . "

The **Thousand Years** of peace

"Millennium" is the English word for one thousand years, formed from two Latin words, *mille*, thousand, and *annum*, year, which has come to be applied to this time of Christ's Kingdom on earth. Pre-millennialists believe that Christ will return before this millennial reign begins. Post-millennialists and Amillennialists both believe that He will come to earth after it. Post-millennialists expect an outpouring of the Holy Spirit which will bring in the millennium. Amillennialists claim that the millennium is happening now since Christ is even now reigning at God's right hand in heaven. The idea of going into material details of the millennium is sometimes called Chiliasm, from the Gr. *chilias*—one thousand.

Is.2:4 " . . neither shall they learn war any more "
Is.11:6 " . . a little child shall lead them . . "
Rev.20:1–7 " . . with Christ a thousand years . . "

The End: A New Heaven and a New Earth

1 **Cor.15:24** " . . Then comes the end, when he (Christ) delivers the Kingdom to God . . "
Rev.21:1–5 " . . a new heaven and a new earth . . "
Rev.22:20 " . . Amen! Come, Lord Jesus! . . "